SEASONS OF THE Witch

SEASONS OF THE Witch

DISCOVER THE MAGIC OF WICCAN FEASTS, CELEBRATIONS, AND RITUALS

SILJA

CICO BOOKS

This edition published in 2025 by CICO Books
An imprint of Ryland Peters & Small Ltd
20–21 Jockey's Fields   1452 Davis Bugg Road
London WC1R 4BW   Warrenton, NC 27589
www.rylandpeters.com
Email: euregulations@rylandpeters.com

First published in 2021 as *Wiccan Feasts, Celebrations, & Rituals*

10 9 8 7 6 5 4 3 2 1

Text © Silja Sample 2021, 2025
Design © CICO Books 2021, 2025
Illustration © Hannah Davies 2021, 2025
Additional images © pun photo, primiaou, and schiva, all Shutterstock.com

The author's moral rights have been asserted. All rights reserved. No part of this publication may be reproduced, stored in a retrieval system, or transmitted in any form or by any means, electronic, mechanical, photocopying, or otherwise, without the prior permission of the publisher.

A CIP record for this book is available from the British Library. US Library of Congress CIP data has been applied for.

ISBN: 978-1-80065-455-6

Printed in China

Illustrator: Hannah Davies
Commissioning editor: Kristine Pidkameny
Senior designer: Emily Breen
Art director: Sally Powell
Creative director: Leslie Harrington
Production manager: Gordana Simakovic
Publishing manager: Penny Craig
Publisher: Cindy Richards

The authorised representative in the EEA is
Authorised Rep Compliance Ltd.,
Ground Floor, 71 Lower Baggot Street,
Dublin, D01 P593, Ireland
www.arccompliance.com

Safety note:
Neither the author nor the publisher can be held responsible for any claim arising out of the general information and practices provided in this book. The safe and proper use of candles is the sole responsibility of the person using them. Do not leave a burning candle unattended. Never burn a candle on or near anything that might catch fire. Keep candles out of the reach of children and pets.

CONTENTS

Introduction 6

CHAPTER 1
The Sabbats 10

Samhain 12
Yule: Winter Solstice 18
Imbolc 24
Ostara: Spring Equinox 30
Beltaine 36
Litha: Summer Solstice 42
Lammas 48
Mabon: Autumn Equinox 54

CHAPTER 2
Life Rituals 60

Celebrating Birth 62
First Menarche 68
Handfasting 72
Ending Relationships 77
Croning 81
Bereavement 85

CHAPTER 3
Monthly Festivals 90

January 92
February 95
March 97
April 99
May 102
June 105
July 107
August 110
September 113
October 116
November 119
December 121

CHAPTER 4
Everyday Rituals 124

Performing Rituals 126
Daily Rituals 131
Weekly Rituals 134
Monthly Rituals 137

Resources 141
Glossary 142
Index 143
Acknowledgments 144

INTRODUCTION

Rituals are a mainstay of our lives; they anchor us to our location, culture, and society. You may think you don't do rituals and have bought this book because you want to learn how. Well, I can almost guarantee you already perform rituals! Do you always lay out your clothes for the next day before going to bed at night? Or do you spend Sunday mornings in bed scrolling through social media while having tea and croissants? Those are small self-care rituals. Did you get married in front of family and friends, saying vows and holding hands, or have you ever attended a funeral? Those are life rituals, helping us mark important occasions and bringing together a bubble of society—friends, family, and neighbors—to celebrate or commiserate. This book is about these rituals, and much more.

I don't tell you how you must celebrate, because that is not what witchcraft is about. Instead, for each occasion, from childbirth and Yule/Christmas to smaller daily and monthly events and notable dates, I have described rituals you can perform, as well as suggested decorations, crafts, and other fun things that relate to each one. I hope to inspire you to adapt them as you wish and even create your own rituals.

Basic elements of a witchy ritual

Just as in mundane life, rituals in witchcraft are structured occasions that are done in a similar way over and over. A witch preparing to do a ritual usually starts by getting their altar or ritual space ready. The details of that will depend on how much space there is and how many people will attend (unless it is a solitary ritual), but there are some common elements. Note that none of these are absolutely needed! You can perform a ritual every night before you go to sleep without any supplies, or during a walk on the beach just because the mood takes you. But if you want to be more elaborate, and you have the time and supplies, here are some typical inclusions:

- Candles are an easy way to symbolize the Fire element, and there are often many candles used in rituals, such as for the five points of the pentagram, for the God (often gold or yellow, as the God is represented by the sun) and Goddess (often white or silver, as the Goddess is represented by the moon), or specific colored candles

for the intent of the ritual—for example, blue for wisdom and healing, pink or pale green during spring time, or red for love.
- To represent the other elements, a traditional altar set up has incense as the Air element, a drink or cup of water for Water, and some salt or local soil for Earth.
- Add an item to represent the ritual intent—for example, a postcard of a Roman statue during a ritual celebrating a Roman festival, a blanket to be blessed during a baby naming, or fruit and nuts during a harvest Sabbat.
- Wear clothing suitable to the occasion. In a solitary ritual or with their coven, witches usually wear robes—either white, to symbolize pure intent, or in a color specific to the occasion, such as black during a funeral rite. But robes are not necessary; you can just wear clothes in a color that matches what you want to happen during the ritual, or jewelry with gemstones that symbolize a magical intent (think rose quartz for a romance ritual, or hematite for Samhain).
- Include Mother Nature in the ritual—if the weather doesn't allow being outside, bring nature inside by adding some flowers or branches of blossoming trees to your altar or room decorations, or even simply some pretty local stones, seeds, and feathers found on walks.

Common ritualistic elements

This very much depends on how much time there is, and how public the ritual is—these things are sometimes done in private before others arrive, or just left out from the ritual.
- Casting a circle creates a sacred space, set apart from the mundane, stressful world. Specific rituals describe individual ways of doing this, but the general process is to clean the ritual area by sweeping counterclockwise around it, then

walk around the area in a clockwise circle, visualizing the world staying outside while the inside of the circle remains peaceful and spiritual. If you have an athame (ritual knife), hold that out and symbolically draw a circle with it.
- Calling or invoking the four elements—Earth, Air, Fire, and Water—creates balance. Again, there are various ways to do this, but the basic method is this: face north, and ask the element of Earth to come and help in the ritual, then do the same facing east for Air, south for Fire, and west for Water. When you have completely finished your ritual celebration, do the same, but thank each element and its energy for attending and wish them farewell.
- Drawing down the moon invites the Goddess, or a specific goddess, to your ritual. It is often followed by drawing down the sun, which invites the God or a male power to the ritual and asks local spirits and nature energies to attend. Stand with your feet hip-width apart, hands raised to the sky, and look up. If you can see the moon, face that way, otherwise it doesn't matter. Feel the power of the moon (symbolic of all goddesses) flowing from the sky and through your fingers into your body. If there is a specific goddess or god you are close to, or is common for the ritual you are doing, you can ask them to attend by name. Drawing down the sun is performed in the same way, except you face the sun if it's daytime.
- Consecrate objects by magically cleansing objects used in the ritual, and then blessing them. These include purely ritualistic elements, such as the athame (ritual knife), and everyday objects, such as any candles used or the rings in a handfasting. First, actually clean the objects if necessary—for example, wash them under the tap or polish any silver. Then pass them through the four elements to cleanse them: a candle flame, a bowl of water (or sprinkle water on the object if it cannot be submerged), a sprinkling of salt (for Earth) and incense smoke (for Air). Most witches keep these four things to represent the elements on their altar at all times. Repeat the process to bless the objects and empower them with the energy of the four elements.

SPELLS AND RITUALS

These can blend into each other, and a ritual may contain a spell, but there are some core differences:

- Spells and rituals are both powered by intention and magical energy, but spells are targeted for a very specific goal, while rituals are more about general energy-raising and/or are celebratory.
- Rituals tend to be longer than spells.
- Rituals almost always include an incantation or prayer and verbal component, but may or may not have a physical component, and even if they do, it's often as decoration and to strengthen the ritual, rather than the focus. Spells usually have a physical component—a spell bottle or a lit candle, for example—but not necessarily a verbal component.
- Rituals are often community-based, with a group performing it together or for a person or couple, or there is an "audience," like in a wedding. Spells are usually done by yourself; even if you are in a coven, everyone does the spell at the same time, alone.
- Spells can be spontaneous and change every time they are performed. Rituals are usually more structured, and often written down and repeated on a regular basis—once a week, month, or year, or for every childbirth, for example.

- Involve the "audience." Have people sing together, or different people invoking each of the elements or saying words of farewell during a funeral.
- Have cakes and ale. This phrase refers to eating and drinking together either during or, more commonly, after the actual ritual (traditionally oatcakes and ale, but any food and drink is okay). It's a great way to cement friendships and family bonds, and also relax in a more casual atmosphere.

CHAPTER 1

The Sabbats

Wiccan Sabbats are the eight major festivals during the witchy year (like the Christian Christmas, we have Yule; like Halloween, we have Samhain). These are the high holidays everyone makes an effort to celebrate. The Sabbats follow the Celtic Wheel of the Year, but I have provided the equivalent dates for celebrating them in the Southern Hemisphere. The dates vary slightly from year to year, based on the natural cycles of the sun.

Samhain *October 31*
(April 30 in the Southern Hemisphere)

Samhain is the witchy New Year; the old year ends with the last harvest. The word is a combination of the Gaelic words for "summer" and "end/sunset," but some also think it comes from the ancient Sanskrit word *samana*, which means "assembly/happy party," and to this day, witches have a big party on Samhain. Samhain is the most important of the Wiccan Sabbats, because it is said that the veil between the worlds is thinnest at this time, making it easy to contact spirits, angels, or ancestors. Witches will visit graveyards and tend their family's graves or those that look untended as a public service, and leave flowers and harvest symbols, such as apples.

HALLOWEEN

Samhain and Halloween take place on the same day in the Northern Hemisphere, and stem from the same thing (the veil between worlds is thin, hence people dressing up as ghosts and carving pumpkins to ward off evil spirits), but Halloween is a secular party day, while Samhain is a spiritual festival.

Ritual for contacting departed loved ones

Samhain is a great time for getting in touch with local ghosts and departed loved ones or long-gone ancestors. Light a black candle and place it in the window over (or close to) your front door, inviting friendly spirits, especially those of your ancestors, to visit. You can also place a plate of food in the guest of honor spot on your dining room table and make a ring with photographs of loved ones who have departed this world. Ask them to join you, and maybe give you a sign they are still looking over you, by chanting:

Friendly spirits come to see, this house where happy for a while you'll be!

Ancestors and loved ones gone, fear there will be none!

Please come and for a while stay, until the dawning of the next day.

Divination ritual

Light a candle for each of the four points of the compass—north, south, east, and west—on the outside of your ritual space, or if space is an issue, on your altar. The four directions represent the four elements and bring balance. Ring a bell three times and say:

The night of Samhain has come. I invite the spirits of this place, my ancestors, and all of good will to join me in this ritual to ring out the old year and welcome the new!

Family of old, of blood, and family of spirit and magic, I welcome you to this rite.

Stand a purple candle in the middle of your cauldron. If you don't have a cauldron, a soup bowl or round vase will do. Pour in some water around the candle, and add a few drops of ink or black food coloring to make the water dark, to symbolize the darkness of winter coming and how occulted the future usually is. Light the candle and close your eyes to pray to your favorite deities or ancestors for guidance on a problem you are facing, or your plans for the coming year. When you feel ready, open your eyes and look into the water, trying to make out shapes from the reflection of the candle flame that will guide you; for example, one clear pool of light may mean you are on the right path, or an arrow shape of reflected candlelight may point in the direction of where you should travel.

When you have finished, gently blow out the candle with thanks for the spirits' guidance, and ring the bell three times again, saying:

The night of Samhain is done. I thank the spirits of this place, my ancestors, and all of good will who joined me in this ritual to ring out the old year and welcome the new. Blessed be!

A variation of this divination ritual is to light a candle in a color suitable to your question:
- Brown for business success
- Green for prosperity/fertility of mind and body
- Blue for health
- Yellow for friendship
- Red for love

Pour ice cold water into your cauldron around it. Think about your question and future path while holding the candle with both hands. Then look into the dark water of the cauldron and say:

What was now dark, I will illuminate; what was uncertain, now becomes clear.

Answers I seek, answers I will get. So mote it be!

Then tilt the candle so that some wax drips into the water (candles that drip a lot are best for this ritual for obvious reasons) and interpret the shape the wax makes in the water.

Samhain food

Samhain is the last of the harvest festivals and is usually celebrated with a big feast of seasonal vegetable dishes, such as pumpkin soup or pumpkin bread (the orange stands for justice, and the hollowed pumpkin is carved into frightening faces to scare away malicious spirits).

Beef is eaten, too: in the old days, most of the cow herd was culled at this time of year as not all animals could be fed through the winter, and so this would be the last time there was chance to eat a big fresh meat meal before it was salted, meaning only dried beef was available for a few months. As the beef is eaten, thank the cow for the nourishment and visualize taking the energy of the animal (strength and stoic nature in the case of beef; or if you eat goat instead, the ability to maneuver difficult areas).

MAGICAL MAJORAM

Wild marjoram can be found abundantly near the edges of forests around Samhain, especially in the southeast of the UK and in continental Europe. Its Greek name is *origanum* (and the cultivated garden version is oregano)—the second part of the name, *ganos*, means joy. Dried marjoram mixed with peppermint and rosemary protects and attracts positive energy: sprinkle the herbs over a treasured object to prevent it from being stolen or absorbing negative energy (especially useful for tarot cards and other magical objects) or put some under your front doormat to protect your home from negative influences and people and allow only joyous energy into the home.

SAMHAIN 15

Pumpkin bread

Pumpkin bread is a great way to use the innards of a pumpkin if you carve one, or you can buy canned. This goes great with apple juice for the "cakes and ale" part of the ritual!

1⅓ cups (300 g) pureed pumpkin, seeds removed

4 eggs

1½ sticks (175 g) butter

1 cup (200 g) white sugar

3 cups (400 g) all-purpose (plain) or strong bread flour

2 teaspoons baking soda (bicarbonate of soda)

1½ teaspoons salt

1 teaspoon ground cinnamon

1 teaspoon ground nutmeg

½ teaspoon ground cloves

½ teaspoon ground ginger

Makes 2 standard loaves, or 3 smaller ones

Preheat the oven to 350°F (180°C/Gas 4).

Grease and flour two 8½ x 4½-inch (22 x 11.5-cm) bread pans (or three smaller ones).

Mix all the ingredients together, adding a little water if the mixture seems too dry.

Pour into the pans and bake for about 50 minutes in the middle of the oven. The loaves are done when a toothpick inserted in the middle comes out clean.

If you used a fresh pumpkin, dry the seeds in the still-warm oven and use a few of them to decorate the pumpkin bread with pentagram shapes!

Samhain decorations

Samhain is probably the easiest Wiccan festival to decorate for, because so many of the mundane Halloween decorations are witchy in origin. Set up the altar with seasonal fruit and veggies, such as pumpkins, apples, and squash, along with bones or skull decorations to honor death and our belief that death—physical or spiritual—is nothing to be feared, as we believe in rebirth and new opportunities through it.

Decorate your altar with apples in early October, and use them for fortune telling after your Samhain ritual, as Samhain is the witchy New Year and so typically a time to look into the future/next year. Peel an apple in one long spiral, then throw the peel over your left shoulder and interpret the shape the peel makes on the ground. Use a red apple to divine your fortune about love, yellow for friendship, or green to find out your business and financial future.

Samhain crafts

Go for a walk and gather some colorful leaves and nuts. It is said that plants near a crossroads hold special magical power, as the worlds between spirit and the mundane cross there too. Make garlands with the leaves (green for prosperity, red for passion, yellow for friendship), perhaps adding some berries (purple for occult knowledge, blue for wisdom) and nuts (brown for abundance), and hang them over doorways and along furniture. If you use seeds, fruits, and nuts, hang them outside after your ritual for the birds to enjoy!

For outside or a larger indoor room, carve jack-o-lanterns—nowadays these are usually pumpkins, but if you want to be traditional, use turnips. Carve scary faces to deter malicious spirits, and happy faces to attract friendly spirits.

YULE: WINTER SOLSTICE *December 21*
(June 21 in the Southern Hemisphere)

Yule is celebrated by welcoming the newborn Sun God, born clothed in a snowy coat to the Moon Goddess, at dawn. Wiccans often have a ritual cleansing bath with jasmine flowers (symbolic of the Moon Goddess). This is a powerful time for rebirth rituals, especially when a quick ending and new beginning is needed, such as to end an abusive relationship, or when moving far away. We exchange presents of food and spiritual enrichment, too, because in the old times, each family was limited in what they'd have to eat for the last few months once harvests were over, and so exchanging foods brought some variety to the dinner table. Evenings in winter are also a good time to learn more about your religion and spirituality, as you cannot go outside for long because of the shorter days.

Candle ritual for change

Light candles in yellow or gold (for the Sun), green (for Earth and a positive future), and blue or silver (for the Moon), as well as in black (for the eclipse and protection) and white (for light and positive energy), arranged in the shape of a pentagram. If you cannot find all the colors, simply use white candles and color them with a marker or tie a ribbon of the correct color at the base.

Meditate on the need for change, and what you are going to do in the mundane world to help it and bring hope and rebirth to your life. Ask your ancestors for help, as well as your patron deity or a lunar goddess, such as Hecate, Rahu, or Isis. It may help to make a list of ideas you come up with.

Light the candles once a week until you feel comfortable with the changes you've made to your life.

Renewal ritual

Take a shower to cleanse yourself spiritually and physically from the darkness, stress, and negativity of the dark winter season. At dawn in a dark room while holding a candle, say:

This is the winter solstice, the sun is gone. Darkness reigns supreme, but not for long!

Look toward where the moon is or would be and say:

Mother Goddess, Moon Goddess, you are giving birth to the Sun God. The presence of the glowing moon in the dark night sky always reminds us of hope, and light to come.

Light the candle in front of a window facing the sun, or go outside if it is not too cold, and say:

The darkness gives way to light; soon the Sun God, born today, will shine bright!

Then have something to eat, ideally something given to you by someone else, to symbolize strengthening yourself just as the Sun God is getting stronger.

AMAZING AMBER

Wear an amber pendant to parties to absorb negative energy and stress, hung on a gold chain to represent the Sun God's energy and inner strength, to stay strong when people are griping or gossiping—we all know how those family gatherings can have the potential for arguments!

Yule food

On cold evenings or before stressful holiday gatherings, drink a cup of tea made with chamomile (to calm and bring peace) and vervain (to relieve stress and aid sleep), and stir in a teaspoon of honey clockwise to remind you of the sweet, positive aspects of this season while chanting:

*Sweetness and light,
the season's delight!*

*A spiritual time I'll have, and fun,
celebrating Christmas, Hanukkah,
or the birth of the sun!*

Peppermint is also popular for this holiday. Add it to hot chocolate or make a peppermint chocolate Yule log. You can also make a peppermint candy cane decoration for your door or altar by connecting ten candy canes in the shape of a witchy pentagram.

For a quick and easy present, get some white peppermint sweets (white for peace). Leave them out in the sunlight to gain the Sun God's strength and blessing, and out in the moonlight to gain the Moon Goddess' love and blessing.

Yule decorations

It's great to make decorations that honor your spirituality as well as Christmas, in case your family celebrates that and you are in the Northern Hemisphere, while also serving Mother Nature. Make a garland by threading alternate pieces of popcorn (white, for the Goddess) and dried cranberries or redcurrants (red and round, for the Sun God) onto a cord and hang them around the house—then, after New Year, hang them in your garden or a park for the birds to eat.

Peppermint fudge

This makes an ideal present or a sweet treat to share among friends and family.

Cooking spray oil or butter

3⅓ cups (500 g) white or semisweet (dark) chocolate chips (or half and half)

14-oz can (400 g) sweetened condensed milk

¼–½ teaspoon peppermint essence (optional)

Handful of crushed peppermint sweets (white or red)

Makes 16 squares

Line an 8-x-8-inch (20-x-20-cm) baking sheet with aluminum foil and smooth it out, then grease it with cooking spray or a little butter.

Add the chocolate chips and condensed milk to a pan and warm gently to combine. If you like a strong peppermint flavor, add some peppermint essence to the mixture.

When everything is melted, pour immediately into the pan and smooth the surface. Top with the crushed sweets.

Leave to cool outside or in the refrigerator for 2–3 hours, then cut into 16 squares.

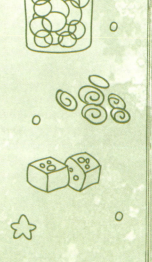

YULE: WINTER SOLSTICE

You could also make a pentagram out of five cinnamon sticks as a simple magical decoration for your door, cubicle wall at work, or Christmas/Yule tree. You can tie the sticks with a colored yarn appropriate to what you want to achieve, for example:
- Red to increase passion in your romantic relationship
- Green to increase financial success
- Blue to help heal mind and body and prevent further illnesses

Mistletoe is the traditional Christmas plant, and also sacred to Druids, representing fertility (hence kissing under the mistletoe). In the old days, mistletoe was collected under a waxing moon and then fed to farm animals to ensure healthy babies would be born in spring. Mistletoe is poisonous, so I would not recommend eating it, but do go for a walk and try to find some to decorate your home—many greengrocers sell it at this time of year. Hang it over the doorway to draw love to you, leave it under the bed to help you conceive, or make a circle with a few small branches of mistletoe to surround a symbol of something you want to draw fertility and abundance to, such as a pound coin for money, or a sample of your writing if you'd like to get it published.

Yule crafts

Dip ping-pong balls in glue, then roll them in gold, orange, and red sparkles or sequins to make handmade baubles representing the Sun God! You can place them as table decorations or hang them on the Christmas tree (an ancient Pagan symbol—the evergreen symbolizes the circle of life and rebirth).

FINISHING TOUCHES

If you don't mind a little mess, some colored confetti can be a fun surprise when presents are opened (pink or red for the friend looking for love, blue for the sick relative, multicolored for someone who needs cheering up). A couple of drops of a suitable essential oil on the gift tag, or sprinkled on the present itself when possible, is also an option: choose basil for the friend who spent too much on Christmas and is now broke, lemongrass or geranium for the family members you hope will not fight this holiday season, or rose or vanilla for the two friends you are trying to bring together.

Make all your presents a little witchy, even those you give on December 25 to non-Wiccans:
- Use a wide silver or white ribbon to represent the Mother Goddess and a thin gold ribbon or a small gold bauble to represent the reborn Sun God to tie your presents.
- If a friend really wants to find love, consider giving them a rose quartz, maybe set in a piece of jewelry—even if they do not know it represents love, it will draw loving energies to them.
- If an elderly relative has difficulty with their health during these cold and damp days, give them a blue jumper or any present wrapped in blue wrapping paper, as that color represents healing.

IMBOLC *Evening of February 1*
(August 1 in the Southern Hemisphere)

The name of this Sabbat comes from the Gaelic *oimelc*, which means "milk of a ewe," as this was the time the first lambs were born. Imbolc is also called Candlemas, the time when candles for the year are made and consecrated, and we see a marked increase of natural light. This is a fire festival, and its patron saint is Brigit, who started off as a Pagan goddess. Brigit is the daughter of the Dagda, the Irish equivalent of the uber god Zeus. She was born just as the sun started glowing at the horizon one morning, and thus has rays of sunshine coming from her head; traditionally, she is always depicted with flaming red hair. Brigit had no mother—or at least her mother is not mentioned as a major figure in mythology—and her father fed her milk from a sacred white cow from the Otherworld (where spirits live). Later the goddess kept bees there who would bring their magical honey to Earth, so Brigit could make beeswax candles—hence candles, especially beeswax candles, are sacred to her.

Peace ritual

To increase peace in your family and promote healthy relationships, leave the windows and doors open for a few minutes as you visualize all negativity and stress going away. You can even shout for particular problems to leave or make shooing motions. Then bring some snowdrops inside (or a photo if you cannot find the real thing) and place them in the room where most arguments happen. Every morning, chant these words six times (get family members to join in if you can!):

Come peace and content—strive and stress, away I send!

Touch the snowdrops, then your forehead, mouth, and heart, and say:

*I will think positive thoughts, I will speak no evil,
peace will be in my heart!*

Fire ritual to honor Brigit

Perform this ritual by an outside bonfire or at home near the fireplace if you have one. If not, put a few big candles on your altar. Hold your hands toward the fire and say:

The chill is still in the air, but soon the weather will be fair.

Fire warms me and mine, I ask goddess Brigit for her blessing divine!

Look into the fire and say:

I call upon fire to melt away the snow and the cold!

I call upon fire to bring light and new life!

Pass your hands over the flames and say:

I call upon fire to purify me, I call upon fire to bless me!

If you need inspiration, be that to figure out what job you want, designing birthday cards, or how to write ads for selling your home, light a red candle to Brigit at the end of this ritual and say:

O great Brigit who tends the fires, I bid you return and me inspire!

I keep your flame, oh goddess bright— shine your blessing on me tonight!

Imbolc food

The main foods at Imbolc tend to be breads and cakes. In the old days, making bread used up grain that might have been starting to spoil during the wet season. Eggs and milk started to be available again around the same time, so it was a good chance to make cakes, too. Braided bread is popular to symbolize the goddess Brigit, with four strands to symbolize the four elements and sometimes sprinkled with seeds to ask the deities for blessings in the upcoming growing season.

Baked custard

Egg custard is traditional at Imbolc because it represents the white Winter Goddess, but also because the golden color, once baked, symbolizes the Sun God that warms spring and brings hope. Imbolc is also the time when lambs are born, so ewes produce milk that can be used to make the custard.

3 eggs

1 US pint (500 ml) whole milk—sheep's milk if you can get it

½ cup (100 g) granulated sugar

½ teaspoon nutmeg

½ teaspoon cinnamon

½ teaspoon vanilla extract

Pinch of salt

Brown sugar, to decorate

Makes 8

Preheat the oven to 350°F (180°C/Gas 4).

Mix all the ingredients, apart from the brown sugar, until well combined and pour into eight 4-inch (10-cm) ramekins.

Place the ramekins into a baking pan and pour hot water into the pan around them. Bake for 1 hour or until slightly browned on top.

Remove and decorate with brown sugar sprinkled in the shape of a pentagram.

HOMEMADE BUTTER

Why not try making your own butter? Let heavy whipping cream sit out overnight, ideally where it can catch the moonlight and thus the power and blessing of the Moon Goddess. Fill a glass jar with the cream and a pinch of salt. Seal the jar tightly and shake it for 20–30 minutes—if you have kids or a coven, get them involved! The cream will start to form yellowish clumps—that is your butter! Remove the clumps and, if you like, add some herbs, thinly chopped scallions (spring onions), or honey. You can keep shaking the jar to get more butter. It is best used the day of making but can be kept in the same jar that made it in the refrigerator for a week or so.

Then, of course, there is lamb, roasted over a firepit or, more likely in modern days, chunks of lamb in a barley soup (representing having plenty) or a nice rack of lamb, prepared with rosemary (to banish negative energy from the winter season) and bay leaves (for money and attracting success in general).

Imbolc decorations

This is the season for snowdrops, which often rear their head around this witchy festival of the mundane year and can be seen until the next one (the Spring Equinox—see page 30). Bring some snowdrops in a vase into your home and set them on the altar during Imbolc rituals. If you need to work longer magic, such as to accept yourself and increase self-love or work toward a promotion, start it when you see the first snowdrop and end it at the Equinox, when everything is in balance.

Use red and orange candles, potpourri, or ribbons to symbolize fire when decorating your home and altar. To symbolize the lamb, wear woolen clothing, or if you have a manger scene at Christmas, use the lamb/sheep from that on your altar.

Imbolc crafts

The Brigit's cross with its four equal arms teaches us that all four elements are equally important, even to a fire goddess. Make one at Imbolc and hang it over your bed or stove to gain Brigit's blessing and have her inspire you through the year.

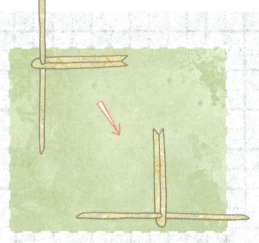

1 Get several pieces (16 is the traditional number, but you can use as many as you want as long as the number is divisible by 4) of straw or stiff yellow or red thin lengths of paper of equal length (28 inches/70 cm is the traditional length).

2 Hold one straw upright in front of you—this will be the center of the cross. Fold a second straw around the middle of the center straw so that it opens to the right, and pull it tight. Rotate the straw 90 degrees to your left. The folded straw should now be facing up.

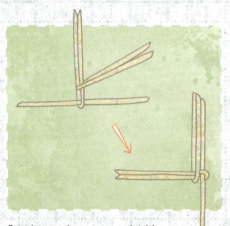

3 Take another straw and fold it around the second straw, so that it opens to the right, and pull tight. Rotate another 90 degrees.

4 Fold another straw over the third straw so that it opens to the right and pull it tight.

5 Repeat until you have used all your straw or paper, then bind each of the four ends of the cross with thin ribbon or cord. (You can choose a color of ribbon suitable to your magical work, such as orange for inspiration about justice, blue for healing, green for fertility, and so on.)

Traditionally, candles for the year's magical work are made in preparation for Imbolc and then blessed by having them on the altar during the festival's ritual. You can make your own candles by pouring melted white wax into a glass and sticking a wick in the middle; add food coloring to make them a variety of colors for later spells.

I love beeswax candles, because they smell lovely and bees are messengers from the deities, as well as a symbol of hard work paying off. Make beeswax candles simply by buying sheets of beeswax and rolling them up with a wick in the center. You can add some magical herbs as you roll, such as basil for money magic, rose petals for love, or rosemary to guard against negativity and bad dreams.

Ostara: Spring Equinox March 21
(September 21 in the Southern Hemisphere)

Ostara is named after the goddess Eostra (where the name Easter comes from!) and occurs on the Spring Equinox. Day and night are the same length, the sun and moon are in perfect balance, and thus this is a good time to bring your own life into balance. Take stock a few days beforehand, and if you feel something is unbalanced in your life—such as working too much with not enough time for your friends or family, or giving too much without getting anything in return—address this at the Sabbat. You can ask coven members or friends for suggestions (and ask them to remind you if you yet again cancel a social event because you are working late), or do a visualization where you see yourself in perfect balance, at the center of a pentagram, to help you feel less stressed and more balanced.

DAFFODILS

The daffodil symbolizes hope and renewal, as well as rebirth, being the ultimate spring flower, sacred to the goddess Ostara. Its sap was long considered to have healing and cleansing powers (probably because it deters wild animals), but nowadays this is more symbolic. Now would be a good time to effect a major change in your life, do a big clean out of your home (remember thrift stores and charity shops are always grateful for good-quality clothes and furniture), get rid of draining, one-sided friendships, or start afresh with any relationship that has been difficult.

Balance ritual

Go outside if the weather allows and stand in a quiet spot barefoot. Face north and say:

I call on the powers of the North, of Earth and grounding, to be with me today and always!

Then face east and say:

I call on the powers of the East, of Air and inspiration, to be with me today and always!

Then face south and say:

I call on the powers of the South, of Fire and passion, to be with me today and always!

Then face west and say:

I call on the powers of the West, of Water and healing, to be with me today and always, so I may be in balance with all elements.

If you can, light a candle at each of the corners (especially if you end up doing the ritual indoors due to living in the city or bad weather). Visualize your feet being connected to the earth, giving her sustenance, and also getting the blessing of Mother Earth—of stability and being grounded. Then raise your arms to the sky and visualize sending energy up into the sky for those who need it, but also gaining energy from the Sun God. Say:

As above, so below.

I have balance in everything I do.

I am content and balanced in everything I do!

Take some time to think about things that need balancing in your life. Make a commitment to yourself to gain that balance, but do not rush it; set a time, for example until the next Sabbat, or until the next Equinox, to achieve your goal. (Ostara is also a good time to perform long-lasting spells that build energy over months, until the next Equinox, and are released and activated then.)

When you are ready, blow out the candles while saying again:

As above, so below.

I have balance in everything I do.

I am content and balanced in everything I do!

Give an earth offering to thank the spirits, God, and Goddess for their blessing and help—for example, sow some wildflower seeds where you did the ritual, leave a cube of sugar for the fairies, or feed the local wildlife.

Bring the candles home and have them on your altar or living room to remind you of the balance needed to enjoy life.

Quick Ostara ritual

You can harness this Sabbat's energy of renewal and spring energy by cutting a slice from the middle of a cauliflower (white symbolizes peace and pure energy) during a sunny day, or at least in daylight, and use it as a blank canvas to draw or paint something that represents a new goal in your personal or professional life. Keep the cauliflower slice in your altar or a mantelpiece for a few days, and discard when it starts going bad. That night, hold the rest of the cauliflower in both your hands and chant this nine times:

Lady Moon, come to me, bring me creativity.

Lord of Sun, grant me energy, so that the clear path I can see!

Now look at the plant in your hand and interpret any shapes in the whiteness for clues as to how to go forward with the goal you painted during the day.

Shapes you might see include:
- lots of cauliflower curls and discoloring to the left of your drawing, but mostly plain white to the right, meaning most troubles are behind you and it is plain sailing ahead;
- curls that look like flames, indicating you need more of the Fire element (i.e. passion) to achieve your goal;
- a shape or discoloring in the cauliflower that reminds you of a specific person you could ask for advice.

Use the cauliflower to make a meal, such as cauliflower cheese, and visualize your energy getting stronger and moving toward your goal as you eat it.

Ostara food

Collect cockles at a local beach (or buy fresh ones from a fishmonger if you are not able to, though a walk along the beach can be wonderfully meditative). Steam them in some white wine (a symbol of luxury) and shallots (the green is a symbol of prosperity, and the fact that you tear up when cutting them is a symbol of having to work hard in the mundane life to gain money you want to attract). Enjoy plain, or over creamy pasta. You can use the shells for a money spell to both attract and keep money in the home by placing a small coin such as a penny in one of the shells and keeping it by your front door.

The first nettle shoots can be gathered in March if the weather is mild. You can treat these like baby spinach—steam or sauté lightly and use in a quiche or pasta sauce, to symbolize money and the balance of difficulties (as fresh nettles sting) and comfort and nourishment. You can also sew a large nettle leaf into your clothing, stinging side facing away from you, to protect yourself from physical harm and send any negativity or psychic attack right back.

Ostara decorations

The obvious Ostara decorations are fresh flowers or blossoming tree branches. Daffodils (yellow and symbolizing the sun) are popular; try to pair them with white flowers to symbolize the moon or dark blue to symbolize nighttime—and thus balance.

Eggs are also popular, and they don't have to be fresh eggs. Make a wreath for your front door with colorful plastic eggs (try using four colors to represent the four elements of Earth, Air, Fire, and Water, or one color going from pale to dark, to attract the balance this Sabbat represents), or get a bunch of old buttons and make a 3D picture of an egg in a frame.

You could create an Ostara tree, too. Collect some branches from flowering bushes or blossoming trees, and place them in a large vase or tie them together with a ribbon of a suitable color (spring colors such as green and yellow, or pastels). You can also use plain or store-bought branches, or even a small plastic Christmas tree, and decorate them with plastic or blown-out real eggs, ribbons in bows, and even Easter candy. I personally love to decorate the tree with paper daffodils I have made and pictures of baby animals cut out from magazines.

Ostara crafts

Bring nature indoors at Ostara by coloring your eggs naturally. Collect some pretty herbs, ferns, and grasses and lay them flat on top of some white eggs. (These will create pretty patterns of grasses and flowers on the dyed eggs.) Put each egg gently into a stocking, tying a knot after each one, so it ends up looking like a giant pearl necklace. The knots need to be tight so as to hold the herbs in place. Boil enough water in a saucepan to cover the eggs, then add a small cup of the chosen coloring ingredient (see below) as well as a splash of vinegar and a teaspoon of salt. Add the eggs and cook until they are hard boiled, around 10 minutes (the longer you boil them, the stronger the color).

Choose from the following colors:
- For purple (the color of occult knowledge and great to eat before doing divination or a meditation), use beetroot, grape juice, or red wine.
- For brown (to get in touch with Mother Nature and gain contentment, and to use before animal magic), use onion skins and coffee grounds.

34 THE SABBATS

- For yellow (which represents friendship—give some to people you want to be friendlier with—and exam success), use daffodils and saffron.
- For green (for prosperity and to draw money to you), use spinach and nettles.
- For red (symbolizing love and passionate energy), use paprika and cranberry juice.
- For blue (for healing and wisdom), use blueberries and red cabbage.

If you have children, they can put their hands in food-safe paint and then hold the eggs to add their handprints to them, which can be fun and symbolize the growing season.

RABBIT DIVINATION

The weather is milder now, so go out for a walk and get in touch with Mother Nature! Many bunnies are born around now and you may see them hopping in a field—you can take this opportunity for divination. Think of a question, then walk along and observe the next time you see hares or bunnies:
- You might see a certain number, such as two (indicating you should take more responsibility) or three (indicating you should be more passionate and energetic about the issue you wanted to know about).
- You may see a rabbit calmly looking at you, which is a symbol that the issue you're worrying about isn't that big a deal.
- You may see a rabbit hiding behind some yellow daffodils (yellow stands for friendship), symbolizing that you should ask your friends for help.

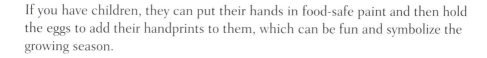

OSTARA: SPRING EQUINOX

BELTAINE *May 1*
(October 31 in the Southern Hemisphere)

The Sabbat of Beltaine is named after the sun god Bel, as we now really notice the weather getting better and can enjoy time outside in the sun. Beltaine is all about spring, virility, and fertility of mind and body: in mythology, the Maiden Goddess gets pregnant this night by the Green Man or Cernunos, the god of the hunt, with the young Sun God, who will be born next Yule (see page 18). So, if you are longing for a child, now is a good time to try for one. Help things along magically and create a sexual atmosphere by drawing phallic symbols on his naked body and fertility symbols, such as circles and green leaves, on hers. Phallic symbols are not confined to the bedroom on Beltaine, though—the Maypole is still danced around on many a village green, with most attending unaware they are celebrating a witchy festival!

YOUR MAGICAL GARDEN

Now is the time to plan your magical garden! If you have outdoor space where you live, great—but it is not needed. You can design a small magical herb garden, shaped like a pentagram, in a large pot in your windowsill with a different herb or vegetable in each spike of the pentagram. Or, if you have that large outdoor space, go with the same layout but with a whole range of themed herbs and veggies, such as plants for money and prosperity like basil and green beans in the Earth spike, chilies and red roses in the Fire spike, and so on. You can also go smaller instead and make a tiny fairy garden with a fairy statue and some rainbow crystals.

36 THE SABBATS

Coupling ritual

This can involve sex if there is an actual couple celebrating their togetherness, but it isn't necessarily about sex or a human couple! It can be about you and your pet or familiar, you and the job you really love, or you and your best (platonic) friend. Find something that symbolizes that togetherness you seek or wish to improve, such as a photo of the two of you together or some hair from you and your dog, and place it in the middle of your altar. Place a god and a goddess statue on either end of your altar, or if you do not have them, a silver or white candle for the Goddess/Moon and a yellow or dark green candle for the God/Green Man. Hold one in each hand and as you move them slowly together, say:

As the Goddess with the God lay,

In togetherness I say,

Bring me happiness and love,

As below, so above!

As the two statues or candles touch each other behind your symbols of togetherness, bring your hands together in a prayer pose, and touch your heart (for love), then your feet (for the work you are willing to put into the relationship), your heart again, then your forehead (for being rational about it), and finally your heart once more.

BELTAINE 37

Fire ritual to remove obstacles

This is a bonfire Sabbat, burning away obstacles to togetherness. If at all possible, make a fire outside at night, but if needed, a large red candle inside will do. Say the words:

Earth, Air, Fire, Water. The elements come together, as I seek togetherness!

Add a little salt (for the Earth element) to some water and sprinkle it into the fire, adding some aromatic woods (or incense if you're inside) to make the fire smell nice and symbolize the Air element. Say again:

Earth, Air, Fire, Water. The elements come together, as I seek togetherness!

Jump over a bonfire (or a red candle placed in the south part of your home if a fire is not possible—be careful the candle is stable!) to magically burn away negativity and obstacles and bring you luck and prosperity in the coming season. If you have a partner, or want to cement a friendship, you can jump together.

Douse the fire or blow out the candle while visualizing any obstacles in your way and say:

As the fire wanes, the Lord and Lady's power remains;

On this blessed Beltaine, Lord and Lady, remove this bane!

Beltaine food

Fresh, local asparagus season! This yummy, phallic-shaped veggie is an aphrodisiac and great to eat before a fun night in bed, symbolizing vigor and a potent male god coupling with the Earth Goddess, or before any work that needs a lot of self-confidence and energy. You can even place the asparagus on your plate in a pentagram shape. Make bechamel or another white or cream sauce to symbolize the Goddess, add some red pepper to literally and magically "spice things up," and if you are with your partner, feed each other the asparagus spears to mix your loving and sexual energies together.

We also see a lot of tree blossoms at this time, and their delicate petals of white (for pure energy) and pink (for romantic love) are ideal for love magic throughout the year. Plus, most of them are edible! Collect apple or cherry blossoms and freeze them in ice cubes for magical drinks and witchy parties, or make candied blossoms: beat an egg white, gently paint the blossoms with it, then sprinkle very fine sugar over them and let them dry before keeping them in an airtight container. You can use your candied blossoms to decorate cakes and other desserts and encourage love in your partner later in the year.

Beltaine decorations

Bring greenery (green symbolizes prosperity and fertility in a general sense, rather than just "having a baby") and delicate pink blossoms (to symbolize romantic love) into the house to celebrate the marriage of the God and Goddess; tie them together with a red ribbon for passionate love and virility.

Decorate your altar with symbols of fertility and virility, too. This can be as simple as some seeds you later plant in pots on your balcony or flowers, or you can display antlers, statues of the God and Goddess embracing, or a photo or drawing of a handsome young man and/or voluptuous woman.

If you made a Brigit's Cross at Imbolc (see page 28), bring that back out and decorate it with spring flowers to thank the goddess Brigit, and all goddesses, for their blessing and protection. Alternatively, if you have a partner, put a photo or something symbolizing the two of you together in the middle of the cross to bring you closer.

Wear colorful, fun clothes for this Sabbat and adorn yourself with crazy, sparkly jewelry. If you work in a conservative office environment and cannot wear funky clothes, celebrate covertly with colorful socks or a flamboyant handkerchief in your pocket.

> **BLESSING YOUR BELTAINE DECORATIONS**
> As you decorate your home with flowers and goddess symbols, chant:
>
> *This Beltaine, May Queen, I ask thee,*
>
> *Bless our way to prosperity*
>
> *So that without troubles or worry we may be!*

40 THE SABBATS

Beltaine crafts

Make your own Maypole: get a sturdy, straight branch from outside (do not break it off a tree, as you don't want to "hurt" Mother Nature; find one lying on the ground). If you are in the city, a cardboard tube from inside a roll of kitchen paper, painted green or brown, will do. Get a white ribbon for pure energy and two other ribbons colored for your intent (for example, pink for romance and red for sex or lust, or purple for occult knowledge and yellow for finding friends who are also into witchy stuff, or green for prosperity and gold for money). Fasten these to the top of the branch and braid them around it. You can add small symbols of togetherness and spring, such as flowers, wedding rings, and so on, if you like.

You could also make a May Crown to wear during rituals or just for fun—this can be as easy as a daisy chain crown, or get a simple tiara and weave real or fake flowers through the filigree metal. You could also get some reeds or pipe cleaners, twist them into a circle to fit your head, and braid ribbons through it, perhaps adding some colorful gems and letting the ribbons hang off like long hair.

LITHA: SUMMER SOLSTICE *June 21*
(December 21 in the Southern Hemisphere)

Litha is the witchy name for the Summer Solstice, the longest day of the year. It's sacred to Baldur, son of the goddess Frigga (goddess of motherhood and marriage), and the fatherhood god Odin. Baldur was such a beautiful and sweet baby that all the deities loved him, and he later became the god of light, the sun, and joy. He was killed accidentally by his own brother, Hod, who was being tricked by Loki. Baldur's wife Nanna died soon after from a broken heart, and she and Baldur were reunited in the underworld, though Baldur eventually returned from the dead, on the Summer Solstice—bringing gifts from Nanna for Frigga, because the strength of his wife's and mother's love revived him.

This is a time for enjoying the sun and preparing for the harvest to come. It is a great time for outdoor meditation, bonfires (where allowed), and picnics with your spiritual friends. Dawn and dusk on the solstice are said to be the best time to see fairies. Go somewhere where fairies are likely (a fairy fort, which is a place where local mythology says fairies dwell, or a babbling brook in an overgrown area, preferably with fragrant flowers present), gently brush your closed eyelids with a fern leaf, then semi-close your eyes and relax, then you might see the little folk having their own solstice celebration from the corner of your eyes.

Sun rituals for Litha

Get up shortly before dawn and prepare something light to eat for after your ritual that includes grain, such as bread or oat cookies. Face the rising sun, even if you cannot see it, and light a candle to greet it, saying:

The warm sun I greet;

Father Sun, I sit at your feet.

I seek your confidence and strength,

On this day of greatest length!

42 THE SABBATS

Look at the sun while it is still barely over the horizon, so it is safe to do so, or at your candle, and in your own words, ask the Sun God for strength in your spiritual journey and to protect your loved ones.

In several European traditions, villagers would set fire to large wheels of wheat sheaves or dry branches, then roll them downhill into a creek or river to magically ward off drafts that endangered the upcoming harvest, representing the Fire God and Water Goddess working best together. You can recreate this in a small way by lighting a single stalk of wheat or small dry twig from your candle, then saying:

Emotions are good, fire is needed,

Spiritual growth is seeded.

Fire God, Water Goddess,

I ask my path you will bless!

Then douse the tiny fire by sticking your stalk of wheat into a glass of water. If you can, let your original candle burn until dusk that day or, if not, blow it out gently with thanks to the Sun and Fire Gods for their warmth, physical and otherwise.

LITHA: SUMMER SOLSTICE

Money ritual

This ritual should be done with the sun shining on you, even if through a window or a couple of days after Litha, if it rains on the actual Sabbat. Lay out a pentagram made of coins, with five basil leaves in the middle. Take one leaf and touch it to the northmost facing coin and say:

Powers of North, Spirits of Earth, I call on you to share your stability on this, the longest day!

Eat the leaf, then repeat with the eastmost coin, followed by south and west:

Powers of East, Spirits of Air, I call on you to share your wisdom on this, the longest day!

Powers of South, Spirits of Fire, I call on you to share your inspiration on this, the longest day!

Powers of West, Spirits of Water, I call on you to share your adaptability on this, the longest day!

Then take the last basil leaf, touch it to the fifth point of the pentagram, lift it to face the sun, and say:

Powers of free will, Spirit, and of the Sun, I call on you to share your inspiration on this, the longest day!

I ask all of you to guide me so I may be financially comfortable and not have to worry. I am not asking of greed, but to fill my need.

Finish by eating the last basil leaf.

GEMINI BALANCE

June is the month of the Gemini Zodiac—the twins. I am not an astrologer, but I like to use this time to remind myself of the balance in life. I may meditate on the pentagram, where the four elements and the esoteric element (spirit) are all equal, or more philosophically, that every dark valley comes with a mountain, rain gives us beautiful plants, and a fire destroys but also makes way for new things!

Litha foods

Have a picnic full of "sunny" foods, such as carrots (orange for the sun and justice), lemonade (lemon for the sun and yellow for friendship), red, yellow, and orange bell pepper slices, and round shortbread cookies. You could decorate the cookies with suns, smiley faces for joy, or pentagrams and personal sigils.

Litha is a good time to gather wild strawberries—small, juicy, and very sweet, these are ideal for food love magic. The best day to go out hunting for wild strawberries is Friday (the day of love goddess Venus), or Sunday if you are looking for a man (as it's the day of the Sun God, and good for any magic related to male energies), or Monday if looking for a woman (as it's the Moon Day, and the energy of female deities is strongest then). Think about the qualities you are looking for in a partner while you collect the strawberries, and then eat some every morning as you say:

Strawberry, bring love to me! Strawberry, today my love I'll see!

If you have a partner and want to enhance the love between the two of you, each should kiss a strawberry while making a silent wish for your future together, then feed it to the other partner.

Seaweed salad

Include a seaweed salad in any picnic to cool you down and draw money to you.

½ cup (30 g) mixed or wakame dried seaweed

¼ cup (30 g) carrots, shredded

¼ cup (30 g) shallots, scallions, or red onions (or mix of all), chopped

1 tablespoon rice vinegar or a dash of apple vinegar

2 tablespoons soy sauce

Pinch of sugar

1 tablespoon dark sesame seed oil (optional)

1 heaped tablespoon sesame seeds

Serves 2 as a small lunch or 4 as a snack or appetiser

Soak the seaweed in water, representing the male (seaweed) and female (water) energies coming together to nourish you.

When tender (after about 10 minutes), drain and squeeze out any excess water. Add the carrots (representing joy and light) and the other ingredients and toss together.

It can be eaten as is but is best when refrigerated—it's so refreshing, and great for after a ritual.

Litha decorations

Sunflowers are the main decoration for this Sabbat. If you do not have an outdoor space, you can still easily grow miniature sunflowers in a pot on your windowsill! When the flowers begin to droop, be sure to take them outside for the birds to enjoy the seed, thus giving back to Mother Earth for her blessings. If you cannot get any real sunflowers, draw some simple ones or fold yellow paper to make some for your altar.

Dill plants have little yellowish flowers which can symbolize the sun. Encourage them to bloom in time for the Summer Solstice by planting them around six weeks before. If you plant dill later, it is less likely to flower, but more likely to give you plentiful fronds for beautiful altar arrangements or to tie in bunches for luck and protection spells.

Be sure to wear something yellow, gold, or orange to represent the strength of the Sun God and his blessing over the growing season. This can be as simple as gold jewelry, a yellow summer dress, or sunflower-shaped earrings.

Litha crafts

Make lanterns to welcome the night getting longer again after Litha. You can buy cheap paper lanterns and draw symbols of the God and Goddess and pentagrams on them with a marker pen. Alternatively, create a rectangular cube frame with straight sticks or branches collected on nature walk, and tie them together securely with twine or cable ties. Weave thick ribbons or semi-transparent strips of cloth at the top and bottom for decoration. You could also cut "windows" out of a box, and make beautiful stained glass style designs using colored tissue paper to fill the holes. Add a tealight in the middle of your homemade lantern for evening rituals or summer parties (use a citronella candle to further represent the Sun God and keep mosquitoes away).

LAMMAS *August 1*
(February 1 in the Southern Hemisphere)

Lammas (old English for "loaf mass," as the early Christians celebrated mass with bread made with fresh grain for the first time on August 1), or Lughnasad for Celtic witches like me, is named after Lugh, the god of crafting and fighting. In some traditions, this day honors his wedding feast to a human woman; in others, it is the day he arranged a feast in memory of his foster mother, Tailtiu, who died of exhaustion after making the fields of Ireland fertile again after the invasion of the Tuatha Dé Danann.

It is a "light Sabbat"—while there is always a ritual, and a serious part thanking the spirits and deities for their blessings, the day is more about fun and games as we celebrate the first harvest. Try going outside and challenging your children or friends to fun physical games like sack races, who can run across a balancing beam fastest, or Nerf gun fights—or tell jokes and play a game of "who laughs first." Then have a picnic with your coven, friends, or family, perhaps with a short meditation sitting against a tree, and bring along foods suitable for the Sabbat, such as freshly baked bread (to celebrate the harvest and Mother Nature's bounty) and fresh fruit. Afterwards, give back by sorting your recycling or going to pick up trash in a local nature reserve or on the beach.

Nature ritual

This ritual needs to be carried out somewhere natural. If you have a big field or lone hedgerow near you, that's great, but a local park or even an area of wildflowers by the local road (ensuring it is safe to be there) will suffice.

Stand with your back against a sturdy tree, or hold a branch or leaf in your hand. Call the four elements thus:

Earth, represented by the harvest, I call you.

Air, represented by the wind in my hair, I call you.

Fire, represented by the sun warming me, I call you.

Water, represented by the rain and rivers of this land, I call you.

Visualize being grounded in the earth, giving you the strength of the Earth Goddess, and gaining the blessings of the Sun God. Think about all the good things that have happened to you this spring and summer and thank the deities responsible—for example, Bast, the cat goddess, if your sick pet cat got better. Think about all the things you hope will come to fruition between Lammas and the witchy new year of Samhain (see page 10)—for example, harvesting the garden, giving birth, or finishing a project at work. Ask for Lugh's blessing on those projects and plans.

WITCHY GREEN FINGERS

If you have a garden or plants on your windowsill, Lammas is a good time to tend to them—harvest what you can to make space for more fruit. You can incorporate witchy practices—for example, use eggshells for fertilizer (white for peace, and the egg is a symbol of rebirth, which helps ailing plants), or use blue (for healing) or green (for growth) string to tie plants to a stake if they need help growing.

LAMMAS 49

Lammas ritual

Light a candle, ideally in yellow or made from beeswax. Place a slice of bread on one side of it, and a glass of wine or vegetable juice on the other. Say:

Thank you, Lord and Lady, for your blessings and the abundance of love you have shown me and mine.

Hold the bread and wine and think about all the good things that have happened so far this year. Say:

Thank you, Sun God, for this grain; thank you, Water Goddess, for this drink.

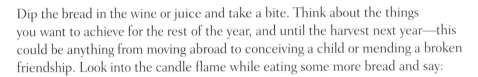

Dip the bread in the wine or juice and take a bite. Think about the things you want to achieve for the rest of the year, and until the harvest next year—this could be anything from moving abroad to conceiving a child or mending a broken friendship. Look into the candle flame while eating some more bread and say:

I ask you to continue to bless me, and let me walk into the future with your strength and love.

Go outside and leave the last crumbs of the bread under a bush as an Earth offering or for local birds and wildlife. Finish by saying:

As you bless me, so I will bless others.

When you are ready, say goodbye to the elements:

Earth, I bid you goodbye and I thank you for your blessing of bountiful food.

Air, I bid you goodbye and I thank you for dispersing seed.

Fire, I bid you goodbye and I thank you for warming the earth.

Water, I bid you goodbye and I thank you for letting the plants grow.

Lammas foods

Beer is the symbolic Lammas drink (although it can be nonalcoholic because it is made from grain regardless), as this Sabbat is also the feast of the Barley God, who dies and is transformed into beer. Beer is additionally sacred to the god Osiris (who died after the god Set got him drunk on beer, then sneakily killed him in a feat of strength) and the Egyptian sun god Ra (because of the color).

This being the grain Sabbat, it is celebrated with bread, too. Make sure to have some bread or wheaten crackers with your meal today, or bake harvest breads, such as fruit breads or a zucchini (courgette) loaf. If you bake your own, consider baking a round loaf and decorating it with a sprinkling of flour in a pentagram shape, or a long bread with grains on top.

Lammas is also a good time to see eels in streams—and catch them to eat if you're not a vegetarian! Eels are prominent in Celtic mythology as symbols of shapeshifting (starting with the goddess Morrigan, who transformed into an eel when doing battle with Cú Chulainn).

Lavender sugar

Lavender is blooming this time of year, and abundant in many areas. Even if you do not have your own garden, you can probably find some growing wild—it was even grown as a bushy plant in the industrial estate where I used to work! An easy way to preserve lavender for magical and culinary use is to make lavender sugar.

1 cup (200 g) sugar

Large handful of lavender blooms

Layer the sugar (symbol of peace and the sweetness of life and problems going away) and lavender (symbol of calm and making good decisions, as well as magical knowledge due to their purple color) in a glass jar, ending with a layer of sugar.

Leave to infuse somewhere out of direct sunlight for two weeks and you will have an aromatic sugar that keeps for 2–3 months.

It can be used in desserts, sprinkled over fruit, or in cold drinks (for example, at a party to keep things calm and happy), as well as in tea and for baking.

Sprinkle some in a pentagram shape on your altar or in your garden to encourage fairies to visit. I also like giving jars of lavender sugar as Lammas presents.

Lammas decorations

Decorate a broom—your magical broom if you have one, or any natural or reed broom (as opposed to plastic)—with sprigs of mint for abundance and money and ribbons in harvest colors (green, gold, red, and brown). Symbolically sweep out poverty and stress from your home, sweep in the harvest and riches, and then leave the broom by your front door.

Why not make a Lammas pentagram? Combine wheat stalks and lavender stalks together and make five thin bunches. Tie them into a pentagram shape and use to decorate your altar, front door, or cubicle at work.

Decorate your altar and mantelpiece with Lammas-colored gemstones, such as tiger eye, citrine, carnelian, golden topaz, and moss agate. If possible, stack them on top of each other so they can "reach out" to the Sun God.

You may also like to wear a sheaf of corn in your hair or behind your ear.

Lammas crafts

To celebrate Lammas and increase love energies, make a berry bracelet or necklace to draw love to you and to give to your love. Find some firm, not overly ripe berries (strawberries are good, as red stands for love, or raspberries as pink represents romance) and push a needle with thread through each one from top to bottom. Eat your bracelet after the ritual or as a bedtime snack.

You could also make a corn dolly. Tie stalks of wheat, barley, or similar into a human-shape and tie it with brown, yellow, or green ribbons. If you do not feel confident making one, sprinkle a circle of grain around a female statue.

Mabon: Autumn Equinox September 22
(March 22nd in Southern Hemisphere)

Mabon is the witchy name for the Autumn Equinox, when day and night are the same length. It is named after the Welsh-Romano god Mabon ap Modron or Maponos, god of youth and strength, son of the Earth Goddess and consort of hunter goddess Diana.

Nature is beautiful this time of year, full of vibrant autumn colors and foods, but whereas the first harvest festival, Lammas, is very much a food festival as we celebrate Mother Earth's abundance, this second harvest festival is more about spiritual abundance and taking time to honor the Earth Mother and Sky Father. That means this is a period of plenty, but also a time for pause and reflection about everything we have, and what really counts. If you feel your life is unsettled, or that you are spending too much time in work or with negative people and need to reprioritize, now is the time to do it.

Balance ritual

Light four candles, placed north, south, east, and west, and cast a circle to invite all elements to bring balance, by saying the following:

Earth, I call on you to bring sustenance and balance,

Air, I call on you to bring inspiration and balance,

Fire, I call on you to bring passion and balance,

Water, I call on you to bring adaptability and balance.

Turn to the middle of your circle or your altar, and light a black and a white candle while chanting:

This is the time of balance—light and dark, day and night.

I seek the same balance in my life that is found in the natural world.

I light a black candle to remove negative energy and what is bad from my life.

I light a white candle to attract positive energy and what is good to my life.

This is the Mabon Sabbat, the sacred time of the equinox.

I manifest the same balance and harmony in my life as there is in the world.

Take your athame (ritual knife) or if you do not have one, a pretty knife from your kitchen, and with it, touch some food you have ready on the altar for the "cakes and ale" part of the ritual (see page 9) and say:

Blessed be this food I am about to eat,

A blessing from the Earth Goddess and the Fire God.

As I eat it, may I become one with the divine and gain their blessing and strength.

MABON: AUTUMN EQUINOX 55

Then touch the athame to a glass of drink and say:

*Blessed be this drink, a blessing from the Air God
and Water Goddess.*

*As I drink it, may I become one with the divine and
gain their blessing and strength.*

When you are finished eating, close your circle by thanking the elements and blowing out all candles.

Adversity ritual

Start by listening to some energizing music or drumming to yourself. Sit in front of your altar and read or think of a story of a strong god such as Odin, and how he or she overcame adversity. Then close your eyes and think about the story, and how you can become stronger and get through hard times, whether due to financial issues, spiritual doubt, or something else.

Light your altar candle—ideally one in a harvest color—and say:

Sunshine and Moonlight, Night and Day,

*Today I seek the strength to fight adversity and return
to the balance that is in this equinox day.*

I rid myself of darkness and pain,

I bring forth joy and positive gain.

*This positive equinox, the Mabon Sabbat of harmony,
shall bring its blessings into my life.*

Then spend an hour doing some physical work (be that paid or housework), then an hour furthering your spirituality by reading a witchy book, doing divination, or meditating.

Mabon foods

If you do not like cooking, this is the Sabbat for you! Simply gather a bunch of raw veggies and fruit, add some nuts and perhaps cheese, arrange them in a horn-of-plenty or into the shape of one on your altar or table, and have both a beautiful decoration and food for after your ritual!

This is also a good time to gather wild hawthorn berries. Hawthorn is called the fairy tree, because little folk inhabit and guard it, and it is bad luck to take branches from it, but berries are okay. Having hawthorn berries in the house confers the local nature spirit's blessing upon all that live in it for all they do. You can add the berries to cereal or yogurt, or make hawthorn jelly: put your berries in a pan, cover them with water, and cook them over a low-medium heat till soft (about 30 minutes). Strain through a colander and return the juice to the pan. (The strained berries can be put in the compost, or under a tree for birds and insects to eat—feeding Mother Nature as she feeds us.) Add 1 cup (200 g) sugar for every 1 cup (250 ml) juice and bring to a boil, stirring to dissolve the sugar. Boil vigorously until the setting point is reached, then pour into sterilized jars. This would make a great witchy present for Autumn Equinox rituals or Yule (see page 18).

SHARE THE WEALTH

As Mabon is a harvest festival, it is traditional to share our bounty with those less fortunate, as one magical belief is that "everything magical you do, it comes back three times onto you." Organize a bake sale with proceeds going to a local charity, volunteer in a soup kitchen, or donate to a food bank.

Yin-yang shortbread

To symbolize the balance of this Sabbat, and bring that balance into your life, bake these cookies.

1¾ sticks (200 g) butter

½ cup (100 g) sugar

1⅔ cups (220 g) all-purpose (plain) flour

1 ounce (30 g) white chocolate

1 ounce (30 g) semisweet (dark) chocolate

Makes 24

Beat the butter and sugar until light and fluffy, then fold in the flour. Roll the dough into a round log shape around 2 inches (5 cm) wide and chill for 1–2 hours in the refrigerator.

Preheat the oven to 350°F (180°C/Gas 4). Grease and line 2 baking sheets. Cut the dough into ½-inch (1-cm) rounds and place on the baking sheets 1 inch (2 cm) apart. Bake for 15 minutes or until just starting to brown. Leave to cool on a wire rack.

Melt the semisweet (dark) and white chocolate in two separate bowls. This can be done using a bain-marie or by placing each bowl over a pan of gently simmering water. You can also use the microwave, heating the chocolate for 10 seconds at a time, stirring after each one, until melted (make sure not to overheat it—you want melted, not boiling, chocolate). Dip each biscuit half in dark chocolate and half in white and let dry. For a fancier finish, use a confectioner's brush to create the wave of a traditional yin-yang sign between the two chocolate halves, and in the middle of each side add a dot of the other chocolate.

Any leftover chocolate can be used in a cup of coffee or added to milk to make yin-yang hot chocolate.

Mabon decorations

Pentagrams are an important decoration for Mabon, as they symbolize the balance of all the elements, just as we have a balance of night and day today. Make a wreath with apples for your front door or create a pentagram of apples and berries for your altar or side table. This decoration is subtle enough that you could even bring it to work and set it up in the break room for others to eat!

Another pentagram decoration can be made with long, decorative grasses and fragrant herbs. Divide your bushel of grass into five even parts, then form them into a pentagram and tie together with string. You could include lavender to promote calm for help with meditation, or rosemary to ease sleeplessness and reduce nightmares (keep the grass-and-herb pentagram in the bedroom). If you include a variety of herbs, you can use them in magical cooking when they have dried out! For an even prettier pentagram, use ribbons instead of string at the joints, in colors symbolizing what you want to promote in your home, such as green for prosperity, yellow for friendship, or blue for healing.

Mabon crafts

It's about time to harvest a new crop of herbs, and thus time to get rid of any leftovers from last year. Many of these herbs may have freezer burn, or not be very fragrant anymore, so use them as add-ons rather the main focus of a ritual or spell. One of my favorite ways to do that is to lightly warm candles in the oven, then roll them in a mix of crushed herbs suitable for a magical work, such as chamomile to promote peace, basil for money, or sage to clear negativity.

You could also make some Mabon apple candles. Get some beautiful yellow or red apples and tea lights or short, wide candles. I like plain white to symbolize energy and the Winter Goddess to come, but gold, red, or yellow candles would work too. Place a candle on top of one of the apples to note how big a hole you need to make, then core the apple with a spoon from the top down until the candle fits into it entirely.

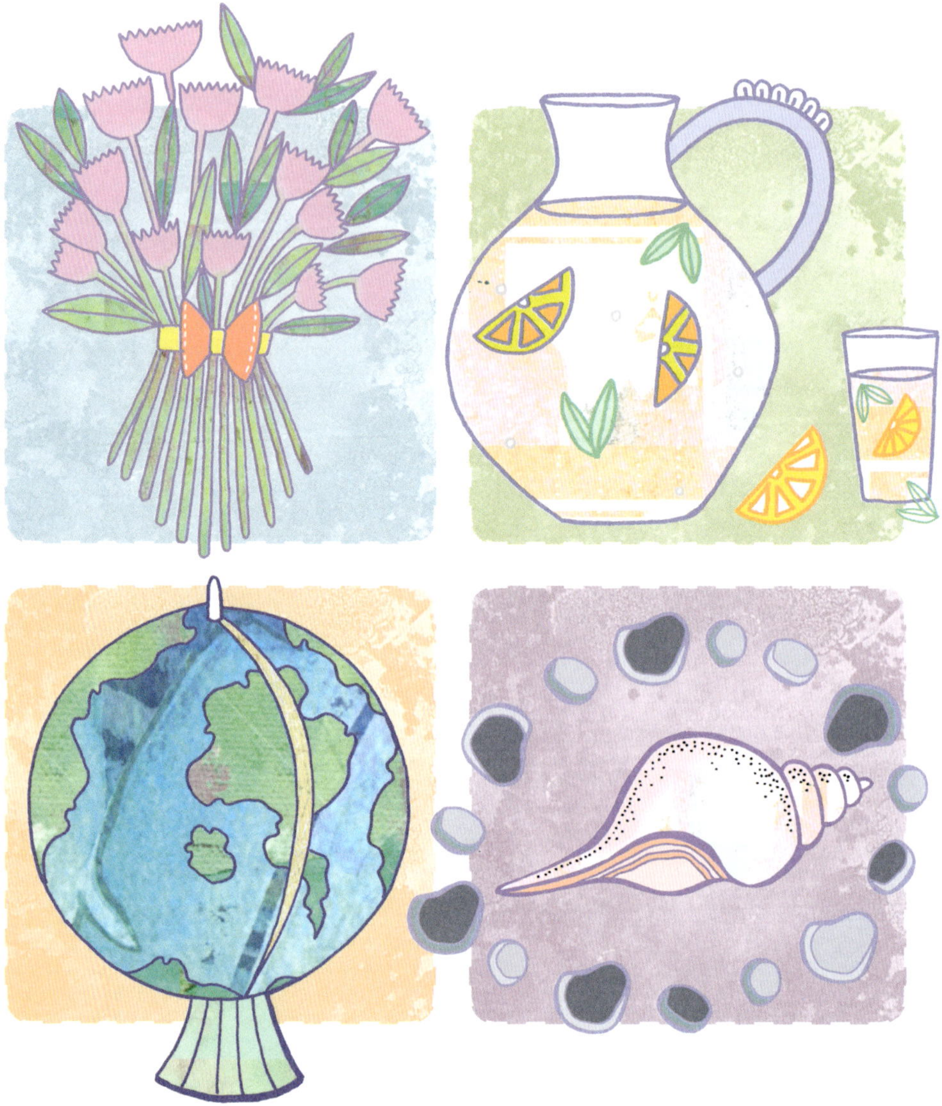

CHAPTER 2

Life Rituals

Life rituals, to help you celebrate and move on to the next stage of your life, are usually carried out with friends and family around you. However, if your friends and family are unwilling to partake in a witchy ritual, that is okay! You can either adapt the ritual to do it completely alone, with the spirits of the land and gods and goddesses as your invited guests, or split your celebrations in two: do the more witchy things, such as calling the elements and chanting, in private before guests arrive or in your head, and call the other sections a spiritually inspired "party." You can also easily adapt these rituals for your personal situation: a pregnancy ritual for an adoption, or a handfasting for a same-sex couple or even poly-relationship. You will learn more about adapting rituals for different situations in Chapter 4.

Celebrating Birth

The wonders of conception, pregnancy, and birth are magical and seen as sacred in most cultures, and so they are in Wicca. In fact, many of the Wiccan Sabbats revolve around the coupling of a god and goddess, and the birth of the Sun God, as we saw in Chapter 1. Women are revered as goddesses at any age in Wicca (one Wiccan deity is the Triple Goddess, made up of Maiden, Mother, and Crone), and this is a special time. If you are trying to conceive or are pregnant, or if you've just had a baby, make sure to take some time for you to meditate and be calm—it will help the baby, too.

Blessing Way ritual

A Blessing Way is a witchy ritual performed for a pregnant woman before she gives birth to strengthen her spiritually and emotionally, and give her some much-needed calm before the chaos that is life with a newborn. It is a more spiritual version of the custom of a baby shower.

Light four candles to represent the elements—they can be plain white, whatever color you personally associate with each element, or the traditional colors (see page 142). Then say these words to call each element (have friends do this if they are willing):

In the North, I call on Earth, Mother Nature, who nourishes all of us, to nourish my baby.

In the East, I call on Air, inspiration and friendships, to help me do the right thing, and to surround the baby with love.

In the South, I call on Fire, warmth and strength, to protect my baby and me, and keep us warm and protected.

In the West, I call on Water, adaptability and cleansing, to wash away negativity and ill health, and keep us healthy.

Have each guest come forward, hold their hand over the baby bump (there's no need for them to touch it, unless you are comfortable with it), and say a blessing for an easy pregnancy, safe delivery, and healthy baby. If they prefer, they could say a nice poem or a famous quote.

Light a goddess candle on your altar, or a simple white candle in front of a picture of a pregnant Earth mother or goddess, and say:

Mother Goddess, thank you for this pregnancy. Please keep me and mine healthy and comfortable until it is time.

Plant some easy growing seeds, such as sunflowers, in a nice pot or outside, depending on the weather, while chanting:

This little seed I plant, may it grow big and strong, I chant!

As I water and care for this seed, may the Lord and Lady provide all baby and I need.

Share some food, and during that time, those present who have given birth already may share their birth stories. When you are done, blow out the goddess candle and then the element candles, saying:

Goddess, your candle is dark, but may your blessing always shine on me!

In the West, I thank the element of Water for its blessing and protection!

In the South, I thank the element of Fire for its blessing and protection!

In the East, I thank the element of Air for its blessing and protection!

In the North, I thank the element of Earth for its blessing and protection!

I am a child of nature, and my baby and I will always be strengthened by all the elements.

Blessing Way food

For a Blessing Way ritual, the food is focused on food that helps the baby grow and the mother get the nutrients she needs. For example, whole grain buns, round like Mama's belly; a healthy green salad (for prosperity) with added dried fruits, such as apples and apricots (for the Sun God's blessing), and toasted almonds (for luck); or even a chocolate cake to honor the Earth Goddess with its brown color, decorated with berries (for antioxidants), and silver sprinkles (for the blessing of the Moon Goddess).

Blessing Way decorations

Ask everyone to bring a gemstone pebble to place on the altar during the ritual, and later make a necklace to help the mama during pregnancy, birth, and beyond (such as raw ruby for a safe pregnancy, moonstone for the mother to have confidence in her feminine power to birth, and amber for teething).

Have guests help decorate the nursery, or if you won't have one, a blanket for the baby—for example, have them paint stars with fluorescent paint on the walls, place a fake flower into a wall holder, or put a small fluffy toy or rattle into a box meant for the baby.

Blessing Way crafts

An optional addition to the Blessing Way ritual is having guests paint your growing belly with henna or safe watercolors; they may paint sigils of love, health, and protection, or pregnant goddess figures, or hearts in many colors. This also makes a great photo to keep!

For guest gifts, create candle holders with dried or fake flowers and gems related to a safe and healthy pregnancy (such as dandelions for friendship, violets for spiritual protection, tiger eye for strength, turquoise for health), or related to the baby (such as roses if it's a girl who will be named Rose). Add a simple white candle for peace and pure energy and ask your guests to light the candle during your time in labor.

Buy a pretty notebook for guests to write in spiritual and life advice for the pregnancy and for the baby growing up, as well as drawings or poems they like. You can also add photos from the ritual, ultrasounds, and so on for a nice record of your pregnancy.

Baby naming ceremony

Instead of a christening, witches have a naming ceremony, but the intent is the same—to welcome the child into the community. It is usually performed outdoors so Mother Nature can welcome the child too, and thus done as soon as it is warm enough after the birth, though some parents prefer the child to have a memory of the event and so wait until their child is three or four years old.

Call the elements, and thank them for the pregnancy and child:

In the North, I recognize Earth, and thank the element for this pregnancy and wonderful baby.

In the East, I recognize Air, and thank the element for this pregnancy and wonderful baby.

In the South, I recognize Fire, and thank the element for this pregnancy and wonderful baby.

In the West, I recognize Water, and thank the element for this pregnancy and wonderful baby.

Have the father or a father figure come forward and hold the child up to the sun, saying:

Sun God, Father God, I ask you to protect and guide this child through its life.

Then the mother steps forward and sits on the ground with the child, saying:

Earth Goddess, Mother Goddess, I ask you to nurture and guide this child through its life.

(If it is cold or wet and you are inside, or you are doing this in the evening, ask the Moon Goddess for her blessing instead.)

If there is a priestess or celebrant, they now step forward and make a sign of blessing over the child. If not, the parents hold the child and say:

Lord and Lady, we ask thee to protect and guide this child, who we name _____ [insert name of child].

We named him/her this because of _____ [give the reason] and ask you to help him/her grow into that name and live up to it.

As above, so below!

Witches have godparents (or goddess-parents) too—usually there is a woman (Goddess Mother) and a man (God Father), but some parents instead choose four people, one for each element. These guardians now step forward and hold the child in turn, saying its name, then holding it up to the sun or down toward the earth, or facing each direction, and give the child a blessing in their own words, as well as asking each element for its blessing and guidance.

Share some food with the guests and feed the baby, and once everyone is nourished, nourish Mother Earth by burying the placenta if you have it (it can easily be frozen), a piece of the umbilical cord, or the hospital bracelet and planting a tree on top, or burying it under a tree if you do not have the ability to plant one.

Baby naming ceremony food

Bake cookies and have some shaped like a sun, some like a moon, and serve with a seedy bread in the middle of them to represent the baby being blessed and surrounded by the Moon Goddess and Sun God.

This is not for everyone, but some parents like to fry up the placenta or make a pâté and serve it to guests, or have it as a smoothie before the ritual.

If the baby naming takes place when the baby is a small infant, guests may take over the food aspect of this ritual and bring extra food that can be frozen or is shelf stable, so the new parents have nutritious food without having to cook too often when busy with the new baby.

Baby naming ceremony decorations

It is traditional for guests to bring gifts to a baby naming ceremony, and these can also serve as decorations: for example, bundles of diapers bound in pretty ribbons, baby toys and chew rings arranged in the shape of a pentagram, or children's books arranged on a table.

For guest gifts, paint little pots with the baby's name and add soil and a few seeds of a pretty flower for the guests to grow. You could also add the baby's name to ribbons and use it to tie up gifts of food, such as cookies or bread, to thank the guests for nourishing the baby as it grows up.

Baby naming ceremony crafts

Knit a coat, crochet a hat, or embroider a onesie for the baby. As you do this craft, think about the blessings and health you want the baby to have.

You could also have your guests sew decorations onto a receiving blanket with you or use fabric paints to decorate it (depending on the decoration and paint, this may need to be purely decorative and not around the baby for safety's sake, and that is okay).

CREATE A GUEST BOOK

Display the same notebook from the Blessing Way (see page 64) and have guests write in it. You can add photos of your baby with the guests, too.

CELEBRATING BIRTH 67

First Menarche

Witches are not afraid of girls becoming young women—in fact, we celebrate it. Getting your period should not be something to fear! If there is a girl in your home who is of an age to get her first period (menarche) soon, be sure she is prepared—talk to her about her changing body, provide books if she does not want to ask you questions, and ensure there is a selection of sanitary products available so she can test which work best for her.

Hecate ritual

This ritual is great for a girl to celebrate becoming a woman and getting in touch with the goddess Hecate as well as her inner goddess, if you feel she is mature enough to perform a ritual. If not, you could do it on the girl's behalf.

Cast a circle by saying the following:

In the North, I call upon Earth: may my fresh blood nourish you as you nourish us.

In the East, I call upon Air: may this be a quiet time of inspiration from and for me.

In the South, I call upon Fire: may I have the strength to face the world and burn away adversity.

In the West, I call upon Water: may my flow be steady and healthy.

Spend a few moments visualizing a caterpillar making a chrysalis, and then emerging as a beautiful butterfly, free to enjoy the world.

Get your cauldron or a big bowl, preferably dark in color, and fill it with water. Put three candles in a triangle around the cauldron. As you light the first, say:

Hecate, I illuminate the past, so I may learn from it!

As you light the second, say:

Hecate, I illuminate the present, so I may live in it!

As you light the third, say:

Hecate, I illuminate the future, so I may grow into it!

If there is a mother figure carrying out this ritual with the young woman, give her first wand or athame to her now, and explain why this specific object was chosen (for example, because of the type of wood used or because it was her grandmother's knife). Using this wand or athame, gently stir the water in the cauldron, saying:

Hecate, wise crone, guider of women, guide me!

Show me what I must see!

Now look into the cauldron for the reflection of the candle flames for answers to your questions and troubles—for example, you may see your own face, but older-looking, symbolizing that you will become a leader of women yourself, or see only two of the three candle flames, indicating you do not give enough attention to the area associated with whichever one you cannot see (such as not learning from the past).

When finished, blow the candles out gently so there is still some smoke—the direction the smoke goes toward is the elemental direction you should learn from:

- South is Fire: keep your emotions in check
- East is Air: believe in your intuition more
- North is Earth: stay grounded and relax when you can
- West is Water: flow around your troubles, and don't take them too seriously

Take some time to relax and remind yourself of the young warrior goddess you are—perhaps watch Wonder Woman, or listen to songs by your favorite female musicians.

FIRST MENARCHE 69

First menarche food

Make the girl's favorite foods to celebrate the awesomeness of her becoming a woman, especially anything luxurious you do not have every day—for example oysters, premium chocolate, or cream in your coffee or morning porridge instead of milk.

Women can do anything, and certainly not just cooking, but cooking together is a very bonding experience that is a great idea for before or after the ritual. Baking something or preparing a meal in the pressure cooker is ideal, so you can take time to talk about life and growing up as you wait for the food to be ready. Stir the dough or pot of food together—counterclockwise at first to remove negativity and stress from the girl's changing body, then clockwise to increase positive energy.

Special hot chocolate

Share this delicious treat as a mini ritual, telling stories about womanhood or strong young women in history or fiction as you drink.

2 heaped teaspoons drinking chocolate powder

2 cups (480 ml) milk

Cream

Red pepper or chili powder

Serves 2

Mix the drinking chocolate powder with the milk and heat it gently in a saucepan without letting it boil.

When warm, add a splash of the cream to symbolize energy and the Goddess, and a dash of the red pepper or chili to symbolize the first period.

Pour into two cups and enjoy chatting and sipping slowly together.

First menarche decorations

The tradition of a "red tent" exists in many cultures to give women a break and be able to celebrate their periods and womanhood; make a pillow fort or other hiding place with red cloths where it can be peaceful and quiet, and let the young woman be alone there, or join her for story time or cups of tea.

Decorate the altar with green (for growing) and red (for periods) candles, flowers, or ribbons and wear those colors, too.

Give the young women something in blue—a new pair of jeans, a sapphire necklace, a book with a blue cover—to symbolize her gaining the wisdom of a woman.

First menarche crafts

Use some fabric to sew a pouch to keep sanitary protection in whenever she's out, such as in school or playing sports. Purple fabric would represent the occult knowledge that becomes available now the girl is a young woman, but any color will do.

You could also create a painting or an embroidery for the young woman's room together, depicting the Triple Goddess—Maiden, Mother, Crone—often symbolized by a waxing, full, and waning moon. If a grandmother or elderly neighbor can join you to work on it and tell stories, even better!

Handfasting

Handfasting is the umbrella term for coupling rituals for witches. This can be done for various lengths of time; the most common times are a year-and-a-day (i.e. the engagement), until any children of the relationship grow up, for life, or forever (i.e. joining souls together so they will be reborn together—a decision not to be taken lightly!). It can be carried out either in the privacy of your home or garden, or in front of 200 witnesses with a celebrant. Wiccans who are part of a group might get married with only their coven present and have a very Wiccan ritual in a forest glade or at home, or they might choose a more eclectic ceremony in a hotel or park where the Wiccan parts are less overt if older and/or very religious relatives are present. Some even take photographs with the celebrant, and in front of a church, to keep elderly relatives happy, and that is fine.

Handfasting ritual

Call the elements—this can be done via the guests, by asking a quarter of the guests to wear brown or green, a quarter to wear yellow or pale blue, a quarter to wear red or orange, and a quarter to wear blue or aqua, and then to stand facing the corresponding direction (see page 142). Alternatively, if there is a High Priest and/or High Priestess to oversee the ceremony, they will call the elements.

Parents or good friends walk in with the couple to show support of their closest people for the union, sometimes after walking around the guests in a circle, visiting each element, and asking for its blessing. The couple each carry a thin, lit candle to the altar, and then light a unity candle together, to symbolize two becoming one. That unity candle often stands between a god and a goddess statue or candle on the altar. If there is a celebrant, they will call on the Sun God and Moon Goddess to witness the vows and bless the couple, and then the couple says their own vows to each other, including the length of this handfasting, why they love the other person, what they want to happen as a couple in the future, and what they will do to make it so. It is very important for the couple to write their own vows, and when I perform weddings, it is the only bit that I absolutely refuse to help with.

The celebrant then ties a ribbon or cord around the bride's left and groom's right wrist—this is the actual "handfasting," binding them together for the time they have vowed to stay together. Sometimes, two ribbons are worn as a belt by the couple, and then taken off and twisted together to make the handfasting ribbon.

The couple jump over a decorated broom (see page 76), symbolizing leaving their old life behind and starting a new life together; guests clap, and the celebrant or the couple themselves will put rings on each other's fingers before they remove the ribbon or cord from their wrists—the wedding rings are the everyday representation of the ribbon. The ribbon is kept, sometimes under the marriage bed in the shape of a heart, or in a frame around a wedding photo.

A feast is held to celebrate the union, often with the couple feeding each other the first bite to show they nourish each other in body and soul.

GIFTS FOR THE COUPLE

As with other weddings, guests usually bring gifts to a handfasting. Popular gifts are two items that represent the unity of the couple, such as a white and a red rose bush (white for the Moon Goddess, or the female in the couple; red for the vigorous God, or the male in the couple), salt and pepper shakers, or a decoration with two cats with tails intertwined. For a handfasting anniversary, jewelry may be given in recognition of the time together, such as the traditional pearls for a third anniversary, a wooden pentagram for the fifth anniversary, or a ruby ring for the 40th anniversary.

HANDFASTING

GIFTS FOR GUESTS

As favors, give something to symbolize nourishing your guests, as they helped nourish your relationship. You can do something as simple as bags of candies in the couple's favorite colors, but other ideas include giving packets of sunflower seeds to grow or crystals that you have infused with god and goddess energy by leaving them in the sun and moonlight.

Anniversary ritual

A nice ritual is to take the cord used at the handfasting (or two ribbons in each of your favorite colors) and tie a knot into it at every anniversary, representing your union getting stronger. If the union produces children, you can add another ribbon for each child and as they grow older, they can tie their own knot if you want to include them.

Some witchy couples like to have a rededication ceremony, where they use their original handfasting ritual as the basis for a blessing ritual at a significant anniversary, such as the tenth, or the anniversary in the year where their children turn into adults. They may replace blessing wishes (such as that the couple be blessed with children) with poetry that is now significant to them, and involve children in an age-appropriate way (little kids may scatter flower petals, slightly older ones may light a candle from the unity candle originally used at the handfasting as they are a product of that unity, or teenagers may give their own blessing).

74 LIFE RITUALS

Handfasting food

If you are having a small wedding, having one of your friends organize guests to each bring some food is a fun idea to bring the community together and have everyone contribute without having to stand up in front of a crowd and sing or give a speech. Having your wedding catered may be easier, of course, with a bigger guest list! Whatever you decide, you can make your food witchy.

Include some food that represents the God, such as oranges, asparagus, or steak, and some that represents the Goddess, such as cheese, eggs, or pears—ideally on the same plate as they come together. You could also represent all four elements over the four courses of a meal—for example, start with Air and a light salad with fragrant edible flowers or orange slices to represent the sun, then Fire-seared burgers, followed by a fish dish or a nice, special drink for Water, and ending with a chocolate cake for Earth.

Handfasting decorations

Decorate the room or outdoor area for the handfasting with flowers in colors to represent the couple. Fresh flowers are lovely, but wooden or silk is fine too—for example, I had wooden roses as one of my bridesmaids has very bad hayfever. As a bachelorette/hen night activity, make flower crowns for the couple to wear on their big day.

If you can, include an "honor table" with photos of departed loved ones, somewhere in the room or outdoor area, so they can be present in spirit.

You could use ribbons to decorate chairs. Tie the ribbons into bows—the two loops represent two parts, but creating one bow from them reminds us of togetherness—and attach them to the backs of the chairs. The ribbons can also hold flower bouquets together or be placed on dinner plates as decorations before food is served.

HANDFASTING 75

Handfasting crafts

A broom is a traditional part of the handfasting ritual. Decorate your broom with seasonal flowers and pretty ribbon in your and your partner's favorite colors. You can jump over it during the handfasting ritual, and later keep it by the door to symbolically sweep out negativity and strife, and sweep in love.

You may wish to creatively gather messages from guests. Rather than a guestbook, set out a big serving platter and some permanent markers, then have everyone write their names on the platter so you can use it later to nourish your bodies while being reminded of your community.

You could also make a wishing tree: get a potted or fake tree, and some cheap plain Christmas ornaments. Have each guest write or draw a wish for the happy couple on an ornament and hang it up, for others to read after the ritual and for you to enjoy year-round. Alternatively, draw a basic tree trunk and branches on a platter, and have everyone dip their finger into a paint color and "make a leaf" on the tree with their fingerprint—this works especially well if there are lots of child guests that may not be able to write yet.

Ending Relationships

Rituals are used to mark all important occasions in life, including the less joyous ones; a ritual can help us mark the event, and move on. When a long-term romantic relationship ends, whether you were legally married or not, you might consider a "hand parting" to say goodbye to the relationship you have spent years of life and energy on. Hand partings can be performed together if the couple still has a civil relationship, and can also help kids understand their parents still love them and will co-parent, but, by the nature of such things, the rituals are usually performed separately.

Hand parting ritual

Start by giving wedding rings and individual possessions back to the person who had them originally; this can be done as part of the ritual, or separately if you do not want to carry out the ritual together.

Call the elements counterclockwise, as you are unwinding the relationship:

In the West, I call upon Water to wash away what is no longer love.

In the South, I call upon Fire to make firm decisions on the end of this relationship.

In the East, I call upon Air to support the wisdom of parting what is no longer love.

In the North, I call upon Earth to underscore the firmness of our going separate ways.

Light a white or pink candle to symbolize the good parts of the relationship, and take some time to think about them, to smile at the good memories.

ENDING RELATIONSHIPS 77

Place a black candle in your cauldron or a pot filled with water (the candle should only stick out a little bit above the surface). Then light it with the white or pink candle. Take some time to think about the fights and stress, all the bad parts of the relationship. Some people like to burn a wedding photo on the candle as well, or in a big fire outside. Cry and scream if you want to. Do this until the candle naturally goes out as the wick touches the water.

Take a deep breath. If you have a handfasting cord, cut it in two. Hold one part up to the sky and say:

Sun God, I ask you to take this and make me whole again. Bless my future path, alone or with another.

Then take the second part and place it on the ground outside, on actual soil if you can, and say:

Earth Goddess, I ask you to take this and make me whole again. Bless my future path, alone or with another.

Close the circle clockwise, thanking the elements for their blessing and strength during this difficult time.

Be sure to eat something after the ritual, and perhaps read a spiritual poem or book, to symbolize looking after yourself and nourishing your body and soul.

COUPLES WITH CHILDREN

Rather than destroying wedding pictures and cutting handfasting cords, couples with children may gift them to their children, with some words of wisdom that while their parents now live apart and no longer love each other, they still love their offspring equally.

Rebirth ritual

Rebirth rituals are performed when a quick ending and new beginning is needed, such as to end an abusive relationship, get spiritually comfortable with divorce, or when moving far away. Ideally, these are done during an eclipse or a blue moon (the second of two full moons in a calendar month—a fairly rare event) but they can also be done at a normal new moon.

To perform a rebirth ritual, follow the instructions for the Yule candle ritual for change on page 18.

Wise justice ritual

While you should seek a peaceful resolution of your relationship via compromises, keeping the happiness of any children in mind first and foremost, sometimes you may need a little extra help with the court system if there are any legal matters to resolve.

Call the elements (see page 8) and ask them to balance each other and the needs of everyone involved in the break up. Take an orange candle (orange for justice), and carve into it words or symbols for the problems you are having—for example, carve a house if you cannot decide who will keep it or the names of children if custody time is an issue. Tie a blue ribbon around the candle or place it in a blue holder (blue for wisdom and calm), and if you have court papers, place them nearby. Light the candle for a little time every day until all problems are resolved.

Hand parting food

After the handparting ritual, eat a bitter or tart food, such as lemonade, arugula (rocket) salad, or super sour candy, to symbolize the bitterness of the end of the relationship. Follow this with something very healthy, such as a veggie mix or fish, and then your favorite sweet dessert to symbolize going forward into a healthy, sweet future.

ENDING RELATIONSHIPS 79

Alternatively, have lots of "separate" foods, either by name or arrangement—such as split pea soup, spatchcocked/butterflied chicken, banana split, and B52 cocktails (a layered shot of Irish cream, coffee liqueur, and orange-flavored liqueur), or have some word-play fun with sole fish and freedom fries!

Hand parting decorations

Decorate your altar and home with symbols of strong single deities, such as Diana, the Roman hunter goddess, Arianrhod, the Welsh goddess of the stars, or Osiris, the god of all living things. You could also use photos of ancestors who lived alone and celebrities who are famously single. At the same time, replace wedding and couple photos in your home and office desk with photos of you with your friends.

Symbolize being free as a bird by decorating a photo frame with feathers and fill it with a picture of you alone and smiling. You could even make and wear a crown made of feathers.

Wear black or dark colors for a while, to mourn the time you had with the other person; follow this up with bright, cheerful colors, to symbolize having moved on, and feeling better now that time is over.

Hand parting crafts

Create things that symbolize you as a strong individual with your own plans; for example, make a collage with photos and drawings of your bucket list to hang on your bedroom wall—things that your partner may not have wanted to do, or are easier to do on your own.

To help you through dark evenings alone, have friends and family write blessings, "go get 'em" messages, or inspirational poems and drawings in a notebook that you can look at whenever you need to.

CRONING

Wicca honors all women, no matter their age, body shape, or any other differences. Getting older is nothing to be feared or hidden—in fact, in witchcraft, being an older wise woman, known as a crone, is one part of the Triple Goddess, symbolized by the waning moon. Cronings are becoming more popular in the world, as women want to declare that they are happy with their age, proud of their laughter lines, and content with the wisdom that comes with age. This ritual is usually performed as a woman goes through menopause, but can be done at any time when a woman feels she is finished with or will never have children and feels older and wiser, slowing down in life.

Croning ritual

This ritual is usually done at night during a waning moon. First, call the elements:

In the North, I call on Earth; I have finished nurturing the young ones with my body, but will continue doing so with my wisdom as you nurture all.

In the East, I call on Air; I am wise enough to trust my intuition, and give in to my inspiration that comes with the wind.

In the South, I call on Fire; my emotions are calming down, and I am ready for the heat and peace of the fireside to warm me as we talk.

In the West, I call on Water; I have seen and experienced much. I am ready to flow and read between the lines and gain wisdom.

Put a new statue or drawing of a crone goddess on your altar, such as Cerridwen, Baba Yaga, Lilith, or Kali. You can add photos of older women in your family, too, whether they are still alive or not.

Take some time to look at your altar, then ask for wisdom:

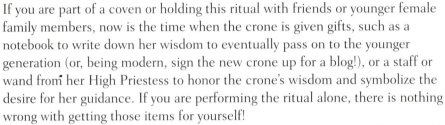

Now I am a crone, but I am not alone.

No longer I'll be meek; wisdom and understanding I seek.

Crone Goddess, guide me, so that others I can help see.

If you are part of a coven or holding this ritual with friends or younger female family members, now is the time when the crone is given gifts, such as a notebook to write down her wisdom to eventually pass on to the younger generation (or, being modern, sign the new crone up for a blog!), or a staff or wand from her High Priestess to honor the crone's wisdom and symbolize the desire for her guidance. If you are performing the ritual alone, there is nothing wrong with getting those items for yourself!

Then eat some food (if younger woman are going to be present, they should arrange a pot luck and bring food—they nourish the crone's body while she nourishes their minds). As you eat, think about the important things you have learned in life, and pass on wisdom to others at the ritual; talk about any birth experiences you had, and things both spiritual and mundane that you have learned that may not be obvious in earlier life.

When you have finished, blow out any candles and turn off any lights. Sit in the darkness and enjoy the quiet, then say:

I sit here in darkness, content.

I thank the goddesses for wisdom they lent.

I no longer fight;

My wisdom and experience are my light.

Thank the elements for their presence at the ritual, and spend the rest of the evening doing something relaxing, like having a bath or listening to music.

WORLD MENOPAUSE DAY

The mission of World Menopause Day, which takes place on October 18, is to encourage women to feel comfortable discussing menopausal health issues and to make menopause a visible public health priority. If you are not sure when to celebrate your croning or want to celebrate a little each year with similar-aged friends, this is a good day to pick!

Croning foods

Celebrate with food that is delicious and aged like you are, such as aged cheese, beef jerky, kombucha, or an old wine or whiskey.

Bake your favorite cookies and shape them into waning moons. Decorate them with dark chocolate or black and dark blue frosting to represent calmness and wisdom.

Croning decorations

The new crone often wears white clothing (sometimes given to her by younger women), as there is no danger of it getting destroyed by menstrual blood or toddlers running around with sticky fingers now. Purple clothes and jewelry are common too, to symbolize occult knowledge and wisdom.

Rather than keeping books in a private room, bring them into your main ritual space or living room, to symbolize knowledge, and include similar items related to information, such as a globe, computer, or mini weather station.

CRONING 83

This is a time of rest; symbolize this by buying some new comfortable easy chairs for around the ritual space, a hammock, or even a duvet or fleece blanket to sit on during rituals or meditations and snuggle up with in bed.

Croning crafts

Whittle and carve yourself a walking stick that can serve as a staff during rituals, too: walk in the woods until you find a fallen branch that speaks to you, and decorate it with your name or personal sigils, and if you want, tie some ribbons and gemstones to it.

Make a labyrinth in your garden to meditate in or create a mini zen garden inside your home with sand and a few pretty rocks in a serving tray. Carry out your croning ritual around it.

Create a new robe, scarf, or pentagram for your altar in colors of white (for white hair and physical age), black (for the older time of life and seeing through darkness), and purple (for occult knowledge and wisdom). If you are in a coven, a braided cord of these three colors is often given to the new crone or sage (a male elder) to wear around their waist during rituals.

CRONE WISDOM

Being a crone is all about walking your own path, having your own wisdom, and doing what you want because you need no longer care about society, a job, in-laws, or neighbors. If you want to wear a long purple skirt and a flower in your hair in the middle of winter, do it! If you want to have your altar with a god and goddess statue in the living room where everyone can see, do it! If you want to paint your house blue with yellow polka dots, or want to get a cool and funky tattoo, do it!

Bereavement

The death of a loved one is a sad occasion, but in witchcraft, we try to balance that mourning of death with a celebration of their life and wisdom (like an Irish wake, with fun stories), and, where appropriate, a thanksgiving that they are released from pain. Due to various laws, what can be done for a burial (also called "going beyond the seven waves") is somewhat limited, though wonderful and ecologically sound forest burials are now available in some parts of the US and UK.

Burial ritual

A burial ritual can be carried out alone or with others, almost anywhere—privately at home before a public funeral, at a non-denominational chapel, or at a peaceful place in nature.

When you call the elements for this one, it is all about calling them to assist the departed loved one, not you:

In the North, I call upon Earth to nourish the soul and spirit of [name of the deceased] and guide them across the veil to the next life!

In the East, I call upon Air to carry the soul and spirit of [name] and carry them safely into the next life!

In the South, I call upon Fire to burn away ties to this life that [name] may still have and protect them in their journey across the veil to the next life!

In the West, I call upon Water to wash away obstacles and give [name] a smooth transition across the veil to the next life!

If the deceased was known to have a favorite deity, totem animal, or guardian spirit, also call them to guide and assist the soul to the next life.

SCATTERING ASHES

If the dearly departed is cremated, it is common for the family or coven to take the ashes to their favorite outdoor ritual place to scatter, or alternatively scatter them into the wind on top of a mountain. Thus, they become one with Mother Earth and Father Sky again, and you can visit the place of the scattering instead of a gravestone.

Light a black candle in front of a photo of the deceased, and spend some time being sad if you feel called to it, but then make sure to recite the departed's favorite poems and songs and tell positive memories about them and about being with them. When you and any guests are ready, lay your hand upon the coffin or urn (or photo if you have neither of the others), sprinkle some soil on it, and chant:

[Name], you were a gift from Earth,

Birth to death and death to birth,

Keep all evil far away,

Day to night and night to day.

Make wave or "shooing" motions with your arms as you visualize their soul departing their body/the area and traveling across the veil and across the seven seas to the next world. When you no longer sense them, blow out the black candle gently, so it still smokes a bit, and as you watch the smoke disappear, say:

Gone, but not gone; here, but not here.

[Name] you will always be in our memories, and in our hearts;

Always loved.

Then unwind the circle counterclockwise by saying:

West, Water, thank you for guiding [name] across. Please remain with them, and with me as I grieve; wash away our sadness.

South, Fire, thank you for guiding [name] across. Please remain with them, and with me as I grieve; burn negative emotions away.

East, Air, thank you for guiding [name] across. Please remain with them, and with me as I grieve; bring inspiration on how to honor [name].

North, Earth, thank you for guiding [name] across. Please remain with them, and with me as I grieve; nourish my body and soul.

Memorial ritual

A Wiccan memorial service is often performed a year after the death, and again every five years. It can also be carried out instead of a funeral if a smaller ritual is wanted, or if the death was quite some time previous, due to the body being donated to science or the close family wanting another type of funeral rite.

Call the elements as you wish—you may want to repeat the wording of the burial ritual, but adapt it and thank them for having helped the dead across the veil. Light a black candle to symbolize the deceased, and a white candle to remind yourself of happy memories and that they are in a better place now. Place a photo or drawing of the dearly departed smiling and happy with the candles. Sing their favorite song or hymn, visualizing the notes being carried on the wind to their spirit. Take some time to remember fond memories and jokes the person liked to tell. Ask them to give you a sign that they are still around and watch over you. If they were a wise person, it may come in the form of a prophetic dream that night; if they were a joker, you may encounter a funny situation on the way

BEREAVEMENT 87

home from the memorial service; or if they were a great cook, you may come across a restaurant that makes their favorite food.

Blow out the candles and say:

[Name], thank you for this time. I treasure our memories together, and I hope to meet you again sometime, across the seven seas!

Sprinkle some water on the candles to symbolize the seven seas and the other world your departed loved one is in now.

Burial/memorial foods

At any after-ritual dinner, or the next lunch and dinner at home after the death and after the funeral, keep the place of honor empty for the dearly departed. You might place a photo of them or their favorite bowl or mug there, with a lit candle to symbolize that they will always be with you.

Plan a dinner including the person's favorite food, but also your favorite comfort food, so you can be full in body and spirit with memories of them.

Bake a braided loaf of bread or marble cake to remind you that light/life and darkness/death will always be close to each other, and that we can learn from both and be reborn through nourishment of mind and body. Be sure to put out a few crumbs for the birds, so they may be nourished and bring the memory of the food to your loved one in the spirit world.

PLANNING YOUR OWN BURIAL

Even if your family knows about your spirituality, they may not know how you wish to be buried and how to celebrate your life. Make sure you have an outline of your preferred burial ritual, decorations, and music, as well as a will if applicable. In the outline, if you have a coven and they are not close to your next of kin, make sure they and/or any spiritual friends who could give your soul the send-off you want are notified, especially if your close family are of a different religion.

Burial/memorial decorations

Decorate the ritual space with happy memories of the dearly departed, including photos of them smiling and reminders of them, such as seashells if they loved the ocean, pale blue ribbons and cushions if that was their favorite color, or things they made—anything from paintings and furniture they created by hand, to quilts and photographs of any children they had.

There is an emphasis of hope and renewal in witchy burial rituals, and they often mention the spirit of the dead moving to the Summerlands—a beautiful place of nature on a different plane of existence. This is why those rituals are sometimes held outdoors, or with an abundance of greenery and the deceased's favorite flowers indoors.

If you want to wear black because you are sad, do so, though more common in Wiccan tradition is to wear the favorite colors or style of dress of the dearly departed for one lunar month.

Burial/memorial crafts

Create a memory board with photos and happy memories of the departed, such as tickets to concerts you went to together, pressed flowers of when you went for a walk, and the wrapper from their favorite candy.

You could also create a simple memory stone by either painting a stone with sigils or the initials of the dearly departed in their favorite color or carving them into a piece of their favorite type of wood. Keep it by your altar or leave it near their favorite place in nature.

BEREAVEMENT 89

CHAPTER 3

Monthly Festivals

All Wiccans make an effort to celebrate the eight Sabbats of the year described in Chapter 1—think of them as high holidays or feasts. However, there are many smaller rituals that happen on particular days of the month to celebrate specific deities or events. Some witches will try and celebrate all of them or as many as they can, some will celebrate them only if they have time, and others only celebrate those they feel close to in some way. For example, someone with a connection to the Roman deities might mark the Roman festivals, or someone who is really into history and ancestry might note days that celebrate ancestors in some way. This chapter presents a selection of popular monthly festivals that are spiritual and fun to celebrate.

January

January 14: FESTIVAL OF THORRABLOT

This Icelandic/Norse festival is a late midwinter celebration to honor Thor, the god of thunder, and ask him to use his powers to part the skies and let the sun through, melting snow so families can celebrate together, and bless believers with knowledge and intuition. It is also a time for young and old to come together, and the elders (symbolizing Thor) to tell stories and share their wisdom while the younger coven or family members help their elders with physical tasks (symbolizing mortals honoring Thor and the wisdom of the crone and the elders). It was originally celebrated two lunar cycles after the first snow, but in the 19th century it settled on January 14.

You can celebrate this holiday by drinking potato schnapps and eating a sheep's head, or any foods to help brain development—try oranges to symbolize the Sun God getting stronger and give yourself a boost of vitamin C! Then play a game of knowledge or strategy, something that requires brain power, with friends or family.

Thorrablot ritual

Thorrablot rituals are focused on removing obstacles between you and your goal and reducing brain fog that makes it hard to focus on your goal.

Cut a thunderbolt shape out of yellow or gold paper, or fashion one with a yellow pipe cleaner. Place this on an object that symbolizes an area of your life you are having difficulty with—for example, your resumé (CV) if you cannot find a job, your textbook if you cannot concentrate on

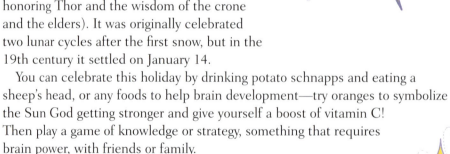

studying for exams, or a photo of a plane if you and your loved one are stuck living far apart.

Place the object and thunderbolt on the left of your altar or a quiet windowsill or side table where they will not be disturbed, and add symbols of the four elements to balance different needs and wants, such as a few grains of salt for Earth, sprinkling the object with water, a spritz of perfume for Air, and a candle for Fire.

Sit quietly and visualize the thunderbolt blasting away the obstacles to your goal and happiness. Visualize yourself happy and having achieved what you wanted.

Repeat this ritual as often as you like until you either achieve your goal or it changes.

Last Tuesday in January: UP HELLY AA

This ritual day started in the Shetland Islands, north of Scotland, but is now celebrated by witches everywhere. It's loosely translated as "Things are looking up holy day," because by mid-January, we can usually tell the days are getting longer, so this is a fire festival celebrating the passing of Yule and the end of winter being in sight. It's a time of fun, carrying torches or burning barrels around, and doing small, harmless pranks. Decorate your home with symbols of snow and fire—cut out snowflakes, set out snow globes and many candles, and if you have a fireplace or the weather is good enough for a bonfire outside, light a fire!

Up Helly Aa ritual

This is a ritual of strength and confidence, which is what Norse warriors, male *and* female, had.

Call the elements (see page 8), asking them for strength.

Light a candle and hold your hands either side of it to feel the warmth, or hold your hands to the bonfire or fireplace. Visualize that warmth, that strength, being the protection and strength of the Lord and Lady, and it entering you and flowing all around your body. Say:

Lord and Lady, I thank you for your warming love, and your strength. I ask that you protect me, and keep me strong and confident this year, so I may turn the hope of this season, and the growing light, into success for me and mine!

Take some time to just relax, and think about your good qualities, skills, and knowledge, and what you want to achieve this year.

When you thank the elements at the end of the ritual, visualize taking the strength and good qualities of each element into you.

January 21: CELTIC TREE MONTH OF ROWAN BEGINS

This is a time sacred to mother goddess Brigid. Cast protection magic on your loved ones (try a circle of rosemary around the bed of a child with nightmares, or a drop of clove oil on the soles of shoes to guard against negativity), but also take risks as the Goddess (usually Brigid but could be your personal patron deity) will protect you; carry a piece of rowan wood to symbolize her protection.

FEBRUARY

February 13–21: FESTIVAL OF PARENTALIA

This is a festival to celebrate and honor not just your parents, but all ancestors, and gain their wisdom. Originally celebrated by the ancient Romans, witches around the world still celebrate it today.

Honor your ancestors by bringing flowers to their graves or helping clean up the graveyards where they were laid to rest. At home, make a list of your known ancestors and gather photos if you have them, then give them pride of place on your altar or dinner table and tell stories about them. If any recipes were passed down from them, make those to remind you of your ancestors, and have them symbolically feed your body and mind with their wisdom.

Parentalia ritual

Light a black candle. Name all your ancestors that you know of, and thank them for what they have done for you. This can be anything from helping you financially and giving you good advice, to having moved to the area you currently live in or given you your amazing skin or general heritage.

When you have finished, say:

Past, present and future; all are important, and I honor all. I learn from the past, I honor in the present, I prepare for the future!

Light a white candle from the black candle, name all your ancestors again, then say:

I ask you all to keep protecting and guiding me. Lend me your wisdom, show me the way!

Take a few minutes of deep breathing and watch the candle flames; you may get a sudden flash of inspiration of what you should do about an issue. If not, feel free

to ask specific ancestors for guidance on particular issues, such as the grandparents that were married for 60 years for relationship advice, or the ancestor who moved countries centuries ago about whether you should move. Your answer could come in many ways: the candle flame, in a dream that night, or the next time you read tarot cards.

February 15: LUPERCALIA

Lupercalia is associated with Valentine's Day and is a festival of love, but not just romantic love—it is named after the cave where Romulus and Remus were loved and nursed by the female wolf, but the actual festival may go back to ancient Greece and be honoring Pan, the god of virility and love.

Lupercalia ritual

The Lupercalia ritual has two parts—first, cleansing, so one's body and mind is ready for love, and then seeking or strengthening love.

To cleanse, shower with a soap with a fresh, cleansing scent, such as eucalyptus or lemon; this also incorporates the two elements of Water and Air (the smell). Think about any negative habits you may have that stand in the way of finding love or deepening your love with your partner, children, or other family. Watch the water go down the drain and with it your negative energy and habits.

Light a candle (to symbolize the element of Fire) of the color suitable for the type of love you seek or want to make stronger (pink for romantic love, deep red for sexual love, or yellow for love among friends) and take some time to think about the love you are needing or wanting, and *why* you are doing this ritual to find or deepen that love. Eat something (nourishment symbolizes the element of Earth) that encourages love, such as asparagus, oysters, berries, or chocolate.

February 17: CELTIC TREE MONTH OF ASH BEGINS

In Norse mythology, Yggdrasil, the Tree of the World, is an ash tree, and the spear of Odin, protecting all, is made from the same wood. This is a good time to concentrate on fortune telling, especially lucid dreaming. You can make a cheap, and seasonal, crystal ball by freezing water in a balloon, then removing the balloon "shell." Keeping berries from the ash tree on your threshold is also said to protect the household from malevolent fairies and negativity in general.

MARCH

March 17: ST PATRICK'S DAY

Wicca has never had any problems with other religions, and believes that nature's energy can be harnessed in many ways. While St Patrick is a Catholic saint, the magical energy of this figure (coming out of slavery to become a strong person in his own right, removing negativity and obstacles—i.e. the snakes—and bringing good luck as spring starts) is universal. Wear green and carry some gold coins (chocolate will do!) to attract money and financial security, or carry five almonds on the left side of your body to gain luck—the "luck of the Irish!"

St Patrick's ritual

First, decorate your altar or a table with symbols of success and luck—these could be personal sigils and objects, or photos and statues of bees, eagles, and frogs, gold and diamonds, almonds, coins, and, of course, clover.

Call the elements:

In the North, the element of Earth, I ask your assistance to remove the boulders in my path and bring me success!

In the East, the element of Air, I ask your assistance to blow away negativity in my path and bring me success!

In the South, the element of Fire, I ask your assistance to burn problems in my path and bring me success!

In the West, the element of Water, I ask your assistance to flow around minor concerns and bring me success!

Draw a four-leafed clover on a piece of paper, and in each leaf, write or draw something you would like to achieve. Try to choose four things that take different lengths of time, such as a week, a month, a year, and long term. These goals can be something concrete, like buying a house, finding a coven, or learning to drive, or something more nebulous, like deepening your relationship with your children or getting angry less often.

Now say:

I will work hard, so I can ensure success is on the cards.

I am looking for success—I will settle for no less!

Put a dab of honey on each goal and visualize how much sweeter life will be when you reach your goal. Keep the clover picture on your altar for a while, and when you feel ready, bring it to a river or the ocean and throw it into the water, so your energies and intentions are released into the world.

March 18: CELTIC TREE MONTH OF ALDER BEGINS

The alder is a hardy and fast-growing tree, used by the ancient Druids after wildfires to start a new forest. Use this energy in your life to heal old hurts and remind yourself of your inner strength. Burn a black candle to burn away damage done to your emotions and energy.

98 MONTHLY FESTIVALS

APRIL

April 14: CELTIC TREE MONTH OF WILLOW BEGINS
Willow wood makes for great wands and is sacred to the goddess Hecate. It's a tree of healing and growth, as well as protection, and so is often planted near cemeteries and new homes.

April 22: EARTH DAY
Give back to Mother Earth by cleaning up a local park or beach.

April 23: ST GEORGE'S DAY

He may be another Christian saint, but he is also an inspiration in witchcraft as he represents inner strength and conquering your inner demons—or dragons. On St George's Day, strengthen your self-confidence by buying a new clear quartz crystal (which is said to bring clarity to its owner), or gift them to each other if you're in a coven. Keep the quartz crystal nearby when performing the below ritual to charge it with positive energy.

St George's Day ritual

Light a black candle in your cauldron or start a fire in your fireplace. Consider any doubts you have about yourself and the path you have chosen to take or the plans you are making, and write each one on a piece of paper. Burn them in the fire and watch the ashes and smoke disintegrate, as your doubts and problems will too. Breathe in deeply and visualize the warm air giving you confidence and strength to forge forward and slay your inner dragons.

April 26 (and week following): **FESTIVAL OF FLORALIA**

This ritual honors the goddess of flowers and spring, Flora, and the goddess of love, Venus. Celebrate it by painting flowers to hang in your home, or pick fresh flowers to bring inside—a traditional way to do that is to bring a fruit tree branch with still almost-closed blossoms inside and let the warmth of your home bring them to full flower. For extra good luck, decorate the branches with little ladybugs painted on, or insects of your favorite color made from nutshells. The week is celebrated with theatre and entertainment, so try and make time to attend a play or concert, recite some poetry to yourself, or enact some scenes from mythology with friends or your children; this can be part of the ritual below, or done separately if the others are not witches.

Floralia ritual

Decorate your altar with flowers or do this ritual outside, surrounded by flowers and blossoms. Call the elements, asking for love and hope:

In the North, I ask the element of Earth to nourish my hope and bring me love, so I may show love to others.

In the East, I ask the element of Air to carry hope in the wind and bring me love, so I may show love to others.

In the South, I ask the element of Fire to burn away obstacles to my hope and bring me love, so I may show love to others.

In the West, I ask the element of Water to carry hope on its waves and bring me love, so I may show love to others.

Sprinkle flowers or blossoms around you (they can be plastic or drawings of petals if you cannot get fresh) in a heart shape while saying:

I hope for love. I surround myself with love. I send out love in all directions. I seek love from all who are willing to give it in good faith. Love will grow in me and around me, as Mother Nature gives us spring to make the flowers grow. My hope will grow into love.

April 30: WALPURGISNACHT

This is the "witches' party" in German and Norse traditions—the night witches fly! The festival has arisen from the story of Norse god Odin, who touched the runes of knowledge, then died for a short time, causing chaos to reign until midnight, when Odin and his mystical knowledge was resurrected.

It is a night of fun for witches, asking each other occult trivia, eating food decorated with pentacles, and exchanging small gifts, like gemstones or spiritual books you no longer want. There is very much a party atmosphere, so have fun—make some cocktails and get your favorite food in. You can easily buy, say, a normal cake and cookies from the supermarket and make them witchy by decorating them with seeds, sprinkles, or frosting of sigils and pentagrams or little witches flying on broomsticks.

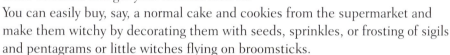

Walpurgisnacht ritual

Before this ritual, spend some time during the day watching baby animals having fun in nature. Watch a TV show on the subject if the weather doesn't allow time outdoors. Remember some of the ways the animals moved and had fun.

The ritual itself should ideally be performed outside. Call the elements (see page 8), and smile as you do so.

Jump up and down a few times, and shake your legs, arms, and head to get rid of any negative energy and inertia. If there are things that are getting you down or that you have been negatively obsessing about, imagine them falling off you and disappearing into Mother Earth, who will take care of them as you say nine times:

Negativity and badness go away—I want to have fun and play!

Then smile and laugh—think of fun things you have done and plan to do, or funny stories! If you are with friends, tell jokes. Spend some time mimicking the baby animals you saw earlier having fun and dancing and jumping around, and visualize that fun, carefree energy entering you.

MAY

May 4: FESTIVAL OF SHEILA-NA-GIG

The UK and Ireland have their Mothering Sunday in early April, but the witchy Mother's Day—or rather, Mothering Month—is not till May, when we have Beltaine on May 1 (see page 36), sacred to mother goddess Brigit, then the festival of Sheela-na-Gig, the Celtic archetype of fertility, on May 4 and Frigga Blot, the Norse Mother's Day, on May 27. At this time of year, Mother Earth is preparing to give birth and the Sun God is ready to warm her new creations—spring is going to bring forth blooms and shoots. However, the Sheila-na-Gig ritual is to honor the mothering and nourishing aspects in you even if you are not a biological mother or a woman, and honor the mother figures in your life.

Sheela-na-Gig ritual

Decorate your room with statues and drawings of Sheela-na-Gig and pregnant women, or fish jumping out of water and eggs if you want to be more generic.

Sit or lay comfortably and place your palms on your lower tummy (those who are pregnant should place their hands where the baby is). Inhale deeply nine times and each time, visualize the yellow energy and power of the Sun God

May 13: CELTIC TREE MONTH OF HAWTHORN BEGINS

If you want some hawthorn wood for runes or a wand (it is good for fertility and prosperity magic, as well as to gather pure energy for a spell and to get the Sun God's blessing—sometimes, statues of male deities are made from this wood), you should gather it now, as it is said to be bad luck to collect hawthorn wood at any time of year other than May. If you know of a place where there is a hawthorn tree together with an ash and an oak, it is said to be a sure place to see elves and goblins at dusk in May.

swirl around you, and the brown nourishing energy of the Mother Goddess coming up from the earth. Say:

I am now receiving the blessing and protection of all Mother Goddesses, and all the mothers in my family line. May they protect and guide me!

Visualize your mother and any other wise, nourishing women in your life past and present one by one. These can be mothering figures in history or famous mums you admire, too. Greet them and ask them if they have any advice for you. Listen if they do!

When you have finished, exhale from deep within you nine times and visualize protective energies and blue light (for health and wisdom) coming out of you with each breath; visualize this light traveling to your children if you have any, as well as other people and animals you take care of.

May 25: **MOTHER OF THE WORLD CELEBRATION**

In Chinese and Japanese culture, this is the festival of the Tao, the mother goddess who is and spawns the world, and is the heart of the world, always beating and keeping everything alive. It is traditionally celebrated by burning incense in front of mother goddess statues and taking your mother or maternal figure out for a walk in nature to connect with each other and the Mother of the World. When you go for that walk, do not follow a manmade path, but instead respect and honor nature by walking a natural path, say along a riverbank or an animal-made trail; this may lead you to some fascinating sights and discoveries, a blessing from Tao.

Mother of the World ritual

Call the elements with an emphasis on nature, and ideally do this ritual somewhere natural:

In the North, I call on Earth, who loves and nourishes me!

Stomp on the earth to feel that connection. Now say:

In the East, I call on Air, who loves and brings me inspiration!

Shake your hair or hands to feel the wind. Then say:

In the South, I call on Fire, who loves and warms me!

Tilt your face up toward the sun. Then say:

In the West, I call on Water, who loves and removes obstacles for me!

Now place your feet hip-width apart on the ground, ideally barefoot, and feel your connection to the Mother of the World. Feel her love coming up from the center of the planet and filling you. Say this, adapted from the *Tao Te Ching*:

I am holding fast to the Mother. She is the origin of all things and beings, born before heaven and Earth. Silent and void she stands alone, does not change, goes round, and does not weary, and is capable of being the Mother of the World.

Eat something—have a picnic if it is warm enough—to symbolize the Mother of the World nourishing you, and then give back to her by picking up some trash around your ritual site or a local park.

JUNE

June 7–15: VESTALIA

This is a festival honoring the vestal virgins of ancient Roman temples and has grown into a festival to celebrate the Maiden/Warrior Goddess and young women, full of energy. Wear white for this, and carry clear quartz to symbolize pure, peaceful energy. If you've done a ritual or spell that didn't quite work, try it again during this festival, as the extra energy may bring success.

Vestalia ritual

Prepare your ritual space with white: white cloth for the altar, white robe or clothes, and white flowers. Get a jug of water—fresh water from a holy spring or clean stream if you can get it, or good-quality mineral water. Wash your hands and feet with some of the water to symbolically cleanse yourself and remove any negativity and laziness. Call the elements and ask for the energy of each.

June 10: CELTIC TREE MONTH OF OAK BEGINS

The oak has been sacred in many cultures and is a symbol of strength and of the Father Gods, such as Zeus and Thor—possibly because it seems to be a lightning magnet, yet usually stays upright and alive. This is a good time to remember your inner strength and stop doubting yourself. If you have a long-term project you want to start, do so during the Oak tree month—plant an acorn, together with a small piece of paper stating your goal, in a pot. As you watch the acorn slowly grow into a sapling over months or years, so will your project grow. When you reach your goal, plant the little oak near your home, with thanks to the gods for their strength and blessing in your project.

Light a white candle and say:

Vestalias, you are strong! This is also where I belong!

Vestalias, you have pure energy, this is what I want to be!

*Vestalias, Warrior Maidens, I ask that you protect my home
and also me and loved ones while we roam.*

Then drink some of the water, and feel it filling you with energy and warrior spirit.
   If you have any gemstones you want to charge for later magic, or specific tasks you need more energy and motivation for, you can do that now and ask for protection and energy.

June 29: HERB HARVESTING DAY

In Anglo-Saxon traditions, the morning (before the sun reaches its zenith) of June 29 is said to be the best day to harvest herbs for magic and healing, and flowers to be dried and later used to decorate holy springs and food for witches' rituals. When you gather especially wild herbs, make sure to thank Mother Earth for her blessing you in this way, and do a small ritual by asking the four elements to help regrow what you take with nourishing soil for Earth, seeds from the Air, the sun (Fire) for warmth, and rain (Water) for growth.

July

July 3: CERRIDWEN'S DAY

Cerridwen is the goddess of rebirth and bringing about change in all ways—renewal in everything, from changing careers or becoming a mother to the menopause, but also inner transformation, such as becoming more accepting of others or shape-shifting into animals for visualizations. Cerridwen's symbol is the cauldron, in which she can change everything—negative energy into positive, magical potions into poison, and so on—it represents the womb of the Great Goddess from which all things are born and reborn again. Some say Cerridwen's cauldron became the Holy Grail in later stories. The rainbow is another symbol related to Cerridwen, representing the transformation of rain into sunshine, and thus the end of darkness and the beginning of hope.

Cerridwen ritual

Call the elements and ask them all to lend their power to the change that must happen. Do this quietly in your mind or whisper, as transformation must come from the inside out, not necessarily heard and witnessed by others.

Light a candle in your cauldron, or a large bowl if you do not have one. Say this seven times, preferably at dawn or dusk:

I need to change, I want to change.

Out with the old, in with the new!

July 8: CELTIC TREE MONTH OF HOLLY BEGINS

Holly is often associated with Yule because of the Holly King, but its month is actually July, to remind us that nature is everlasting and evergreen, and it is a symbol of male energy and protection. You can make "holly" water by soaking some leaves in clean water and leaving them out in the moonlight and sunlight. Use the water to sprinkle around the home or clean your valuables in it for protection.

Coconut French toast

Eating coconut French toast is a great way to honor Cerridwen and help bring the winds of change into your life, as it includes eggs (the ultimate symbol of rebirth), milk (symbolizing the nurturing and blessing of the Goddess), honey (symbolizing working toward change), stale bread (representing what is off and must be changed), and, of course, coconut (the three marks on a coconut symbolize the Triple Goddess, and the hairy brown exterior hides the transformed smooth white interior).

3 eggs

½ cup (120 ml) milk

1 tablespoon honey

2 tablespoons flaked coconut

4 slices stale bread

Serves 2

Mix together the eggs, milk, honey, and coconut, then soak the bread in it while thinking about the changes you want to make to your life. Fry in a frying pan or under the grill until golden brown, eat while still warm, and imagine the food fueling your magical intentions to transform.

Breathe deeply and ask Cerridwen to help you with any changes needed in your life—note that this is for changes *you* can effect; do not ask Cerridwen to change other people on your behalf.

July 18: FESTIVAL OF BAD OMENS

This day was originally marked in ancient Roman times. Be extra vigilant to recognize any omens and signs the deities may want to warn you about someone or something. Take a walk outside and keep an eye out for wildlife (for example, a rabbit running away may be an omen that you should keep an eye on your fertility over the next while, or seeing dead ladybugs may mean that you will have bad luck, so there is no point in playing the lottery) and notice what the plants are doing (a previously unnoticed patch of blue flowers could indicate a health issue, as blue stands for healing; a large tree branch across your path may signal that you are on the wrong path in your career). If it's raining, read your tarot cards or do some other form of divination.

Bad omens ritual

Take a handful of cloves on your walk. You can call the elements in any form you want, though being surrounded by nature, if you are in a hurry, there is no need to. When you find a big, healthy tree, sprinkle the cloves in a circle around the tree and yourself to ward against curses and bad omens, and protect both the tree and you. Say:

Strong, safe, and long-living is this tree,

Just as I want to be.

As these cloves will protect thee,

So they will guide and protect my family!

Stand with your back against the tree, and visualize being grounded in the earth, giving you the strength of the Earth Goddess, and gaining the blessings of the Sun God through the tree's branches reaching high into the sky. Realize that even if you become aware of a bad omen or bad event in your future as a result of divination, it is not inevitable—fortune-telling and bad omens exist so you are forewarned and can guard against any negative events.

Bend down and touch the soil, then stretch up as high as you can toward the sky, and visualize yourself walking hand in hand with the God and Goddess, who protect and guide you.

AUGUST

August 5: CELTIC TREE MONTH OF HAZEL BEGINS

A time to celebrate the life force and survival within all of us. Hazel trees often grow around magical springs and fairy forts, and are associated with wisdom and knowledge, as well as divination. Eat some hazelnuts or hazelnut cookies before reading your next book or studying for an exam.

August 13: HECATE DAY

Hecate is a very powerful crone goddess, who rules both life and death/the Underworld and can facilitate you speaking to spirits. Wiccans honor Hecate's Day by leaving food for wild creatures, such as birdseed, at crossroads, or volunteering at a soup kitchen. The wild creatures relate to Hecate's pack of dogs who protect her and her followers, but are also a more general symbol of the fact that Hecate looks after those that others pass by, such as the homeless, stray dogs and cats, less attractive birds, and so forth.

Hecate ritual

Perform this ritual in a doorway or a verge between forest and field to symbolize being between the worlds, ideally at night. Ask the elements to attend, and to bring the spirits of their element and of nature.

110 MONTHLY FESTIVALS

Now close your eyes and say:

*Hecate, Queen of Night and the Spirit World, show me what
I must see!*

*Bring close to me the messages of the other world, so I may
know, and I may act!*

Calm your breathing and listen for the sounds of the night. Sudden flashes of inspiration may appear.

August 23: FESTIVAL OF HEPHAESTUS

Hephaestus is the Greek god of fire and volcanoes, similar to the Roman god Vulcan and the Etruscan deity Sethlans. They are the weapon smiths of the gods. In 64 CE, a great fire destroyed much of Rome, and it was seen as Vulcan's wrath that emperor Nero was lazy and did not honor the deities, so the next emperor, Domitian, built a huge temple to Vulcan and expanded his festival to include the sacrificing of red bulls; to this day, the festival of Hephaestus is celebrated by eating beef. If you need a new athame (ritual knife) or anything made of metal, such as new scissors or a car, this is a good time to purchase it. Traditionally, controlled brush fires were done on this day.

Hephaestus ritual

Make a bonfire or light an orange candle on your altar. Call the elements, starting in the South to honor the Fire:

*Fire, element of the South, I call on you to take pride of
place this day!*

*Water, element of the West, I call on you to douse the excesses
of Fire!*

*Earth, element of the North, I call on you to be warmed by
Fire, attend this day!*

*Air, element of the East, I call on you to balance Fire and stop
its negative elements!*

Get close to the fire or candle flame and feel its warmth while saying:

Hephaestus, you are so strong; burn away all that is wrong.

*You are not perfect, neither am I, but with your guidance,
I can warm others in body and mind!*

Throw a few grains into the fire or candle flame (or around the candle if you prefer) as an offering and to symbolize the harvest about to start, then ask Hephaestus to meet any needs you currently have.

If you have a bonfire, you can now roast some beef sausages on it, or sweetcorn if you are vegetarian as it also symbolizes the sun. If you have a candle, warm a few wheat crackers on them before eating them, and imagine the blessing and protection of Hephaestus entering you.

When you are ready, douse the fire or blow out the candle, and say:

Fire deities, I love and appreciate you and your might.

I ask for your warmth, and not destruction tonight—

And always. As above from the sun, so below from volcanoes.

Say goodbye to the elements and then thank them for assisting and keeping Fire in check.

September

September 2: CELTIC TREE MONTH OF VINE BEGINS

Celebrate the start of the Celtic Vine Tree month with a visit to a local winery to enjoy their products! Before you leave, ask for some grapevines. You can soak them in water and then make them into a pentagram wreath, including hazelnuts at the five points, to decorate your altar or table at home. It will provide protection from intruders and bad energy.

September 13: OPULUM JOVIS

This day celebrates Juno, goddess of love and relationships, Jupiter, god of strength and keeping you and yours safe, and Minerva, goddess of art and work. In the old days, the table was set to include places for them, occupied by statues of the three deities, and they were served the choicest bits of dinner. These days, witches still have statues of their favorite deities at the table for this festival, but usually surround them with nonperishable foods which are later donated to a local shelter or food pantry to give back for the blessings we have been given.

A feast to celebrate the harvest, this is a fun day to eat with friends and family—usually pot-luck style—and be thankful for what you have: food, money, health, and relationships, especially anything that has improved over the last year. Take some time to write a thank-you note for a boss or teacher that went out of their way for you, or contact the management of a shop where the salespeople were kind to you. Decorate your home with autumnal fruit and pretty colored leaves.

Opulus Jovis ritual

Performed during cooking in preparation for the feast, this ritual is a little looser than normal structured rituals.
- The first time you touch an ingredient, call for the element of Earth.
- The first time you smell an ingredient or your cooking/baking, call for the element of Air.
- The first time you turn on the stove or oven, call for the element of Fire.
- The first time you add water or other liquid to a pan, call for the element of Water.

Be mindful as you prepare the food, and ask the deities to attend. When it feels right, and not necessarily at the same time, say the phrases below. You can say them at any time in any order. Even if you've performed the ritual before, be guided by your intuition on when to say the words—you do not need to say them at the same time as before. The phrases are:

Goddess Juno, Goddess of creation, help me prepare a feast worthy of you!

God Jupiter, keep my food fresh and make it tasty, and protect all those who will attend!

Goddess Minerva, I ask you make this a joyous feast of blessings and thanksgiving!

Encourage your guests (or yourself, if alone) to say some word of thanks or blessing over the food before you eat, and thank each other for nice things the other may not even have realized they did for you.

Do not open the circle or dismiss the elements until the feast is finished and you are cleaning up. Close it in this way:
- When you wash the dishes, thank the element of Water.
- When you blow out candles or turn on the heating for the night, thank the element of Fire.
- When you open the windows to air out the house, thank the element of Air.
- When you are putting the leftovers away (or leaving anything suitable outside for wildlife), thank the element of Earth.

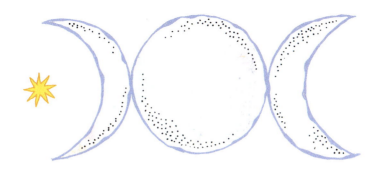

September 17: CUIVANYA

Cuivanya is from Filianism and Dianic Wicca, which are pagan traditions that solely worship the female goddesses. Also called the Feast of All Life, it is a ritual day celebrating the Triple Goddess—Maiden, Mother, Crone. It was originally celebrated in three stages: the waxing moon (for the Maiden Goddess) before the Autumn Equinox, then the Full Moon (for the Mother Goddess), and the waning moon (for the Crone Goddess) after that, but now, with busy lives, most witches have settled on September 17.

Celebrate the festival by wearing a triple moon crown, burning candles in white, green or brown, and black, and decorating your home or wearing clothes in these colors.

Cuivanya ritual

Call the elements (see page 8) and any female goddesses you feel close to. Chant over and over:

"I am the divine feminine!"

Feel the power of the blessings of all goddesses build up inside of you.

Draw a waxing moon on your right arm (for action), a full moon on your tummy (for fertility—not necessarily having a baby, but a fertile mind, too), and a waning moon on your left arm (for intuition and wisdom). Keep these on you at least until the next morning, but ideally for a lunar cycle.

September 30: CELTIC TREE MONTH OF IVY BEGINS

This is the end of the harvest season, and we prepare for Samhain (see page 12) and the beginning of winter, symbolized by ivy that will use other plants to grow, but lives on long after they have died. Use this survivor energy to cut cords with those who are toxic to you.

OCTOBER

October 4: ANIMAL BLESSING DAY

This is a day witches have borrowed from Catholics (St Francis' Day) and made their own. If you have pets, give them an extra treat today or take them for an especially long walk. Do a blessing ritual over them, and ask them to bless you with their insights, too—ask them to watch you or walk the circle/pentagram with you as you call the elements, or chirp/howl as you ask for the protection of the Lord and Lady. If you do not have pets, perform a similar ritual in an outdoor place with lots of wild animals around. If you have the means, bless your local shelter or animal rescue with a donation of money, goods, or your time.

October 8: FESTIVAL OF FELICITAS

This Roman goddess is in charge of changing your luck actively through changing behavior and hard work (as opposed to Fortuna, who relates to pure luck). Decorate your home with a cornucopia of fruit you gathered or food you made. Write greeting cards to old friends and lonely neighbors, and generally spread kindness, so kindness will be given to you.

October 19: ARMILUSTRIUM

This is a Roman festival in honor of Mars, the god of weaponry and war. In the old days, soldiers' weapons and armor were purified by temple priests by being passed through an oakwood fire (oak being symbolic of strength and endurance) while trumpets sounded, and then put away for the winter unless there was a war. Modern witches instead take care of their athames and bolines (magical knives)—we do not put them away for winter, but make sure they are clean, oil any wooden parts, and clean off dirt and fingerprints with oak leaves. This is also a good day to gather nuts, which, similar to blunt pieces of iron made into beautiful swords by a weaponsmith, symbolize hidden beauty and looking beyond the veil.

Armilustrium ritual

When calling the elements, use candles or another light source to symbolize illuminating the coming darkness of winter, but also looking into other worlds so near to Samhain, when the veil between this world and the next is thinnest. Place one candle in front of you and say:

In the North, the element of Earth gives us these nuts to nourish us body and soul. Hail and welcome!

Place a few nuts around the candle, then say:

In the East, the element of Air gives us these nuts to inspire us, mind and soul. Hail and welcome!

Place a few nuts around the candle, then say:

In the South, the element of Fire gives us these nuts to burn away hunger and doubt. Hail and welcome!

Place a few nuts around the candle, then say:

In the West, the element of Water gives us these nuts to help us see this world and the next. Hail and welcome!

Place a few nuts around the candle, then add the last of the nuts into a small bowl. Sprinkle the bowl with some salt and then some water, and then pass it through a candle flame and incense on your altar, as you chant nine times:

Earth, Air, Fire, Water!

Lord and Lady, I am your daughter!

Take some time to think about *your* hidden beauty—perhaps there is something you were good at as a child, but have not done in years because you were mocked for it at the time? Or there is a part of your body that you think is "weird," but others compliment you on? Be proud of your inner beauty and show it off! Pass your hands through the candle flame (quickly, don't get burnt) and say:

Hidden beauty, now I see,

Confident and proud of me, I will be!

Close the circle, thank the elements for attending, and eat some of the nuts from the ritual between now and Samhain.

October 28: CELTIC TREE MONTH OF REED BEGINS

Reeds are used to make flute-like sounds to call for the spirits of the Underworld to attend Samhain celebrations, or to contact ghosts of ancestors. It's a good time for learning and practicing divination and fortune telling and deepening your spiritual connection, as the veil between the worlds is thin.

November

November 12: FESTIVAL OF CERNUNNOS

Also called the Festival of Odin, this day was later made into Martinsmas, the festival of St Marin by Catholics, who gave their saint many of the attributes of Cernunnos, god of the hunt—that is, being a wanderer, curious but never settled, and close to nature. Decorate your home with greenery and wood, especially oak, holly, and ivy, and trees—anything from a yucca palm or bonsai to photos of trees. If you like meat, this is a festival where all kinds of meat from forest animals is traditionally served, such as deer, wild pig, or wood pigeon.

Cernunnos ritual

The Cernunnos ritual is a casual one, as the wanderer did not have much time or many supplies. Go for a walk in the forest and call the elements by simply turning in each direction. Ask for strength from the god of the hunt by stomping your feet or drumming and take in his energy by eating a forest-related feast.

November 16: CROSSROAD NIGHT

This festival is also called Depina Hecates or Hecate's Night. It is a night to honor wisdom, to look within for wisdom and trust your intuition, and to honor the Crone Goddess. Traditionally, black and silver are worn and a sickle and keys carried, as the sickle is the symbol of Hecate's power over death and the Underworld, and the keys unlock the Mysteries (wisdom in general and spiritual knowledge). It is a calm, quiet night: no big parties, no music other than perhaps a steady drum beat for meditation, no TV or radio, as you seek to discover yourself and your true needs. For food, eat things that fill you up, so you are not hungry during the night's meditations and walk. Porridge is good, or a hearty stew.

Crossroad ritual

Ideally, go for a walk at night to a quiet country crossroad for this ritual. If that is not possible, perform the ritual at home where two hallways meet or "make a crossroad" with lines of nuts on the floor, keeping the area dark.

   Call the elements by sprinkling some salt in the north, spritzing some essential oil or perfume in the east, sprinkling a little ash or placing a coal in the south,

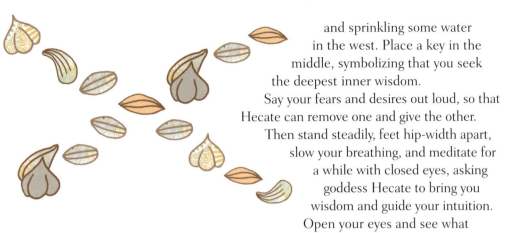

and sprinkling some water in the west. Place a key in the middle, symbolizing that you seek the deepest inner wisdom.

Say your fears and desires out loud, so that Hecate can remove one and give the other. Then stand steadily, feet hip-width apart, slow your breathing, and meditate for a while with closed eyes, asking goddess Hecate to bring you wisdom and guide your intuition. Open your eyes and see what Mother Nature shows you—for example, you might see a penny on the ground, indicating you must look after your finances first, spot some moss on a nearby tree that looks like the face of a friend you grew apart from (contact them now!), or stumble as you start to walk home, meaning there are going to be some troubles on your chosen path, but it is the right one...

When you are ready, leave a food offering for the wild animals in the area, or promise Mother Nature and Hecate that you will take some food to a local park for the wildlife if doing the ritual at home. Pick up the key and say:

Hecate, I thank you for guiding me, and giving me this key.

I appreciate your wisdom and will listen to my intuition!

Thank the elements and spend the rest of the night in quiet contemplation, perhaps reading a book of wise quotes or just relaxing.

November 24: CELTIC TREE MONTH OF ELDER BEGINS

The elder tree is easily damaged, but hard to actually kill—it will come back even from total destruction. This reminds us that we, too, are survivors. Burning elder is also said to help in contacting fairies.

December

December 4: ST BARBARA'S DAY

St Barbara is patron saint of miners, engineers, and mathematicians, often thought as a Christian version of the fire goddess Brigit (see page 24). She was abused by her father and fled when he wanted to force her into marriage (she wanted to remain a virgin). He tried to have her burned like a witch, but fire would not touch her. Eventually her father beheaded her, but God punished her father by striking him dead with lightning.

Celebrate her by bringing in some branches from flowering trees, such as cherry or apple—soak them in a lukewarm bath overnight, then put them in a vase near your heater or any place where it is very warm and bright. They won't flower immediately—it will take 2–3 weeks; i.e. they should just about be ready to flower at Yule.

St Barbara's ritual

This is best carried out by a roaring fire. Call the elements:

North, Earth, I call on your power to make and keep me strong!

East, Air, I call on your power to make and keep me strong!

South, Fire, I call on your power to make and keep me strong!

West, Water, I call on your power to make and keep me strong!

Light a white candle in honor of St Barbara (white for pure energy and purity). Say:

This day, we honor your strength, your determination, your confidence. Through you, I learn that I can be a fearsome maiden, a nurturing mother, or a wise crone, whatever I want!

Breathe deeply and feel St Barbara's confidence and willingness to stand up for what is right, and what she wanted, enter you. Take some time to think about what you want out of life.

When you are ready, blow out the white candle and then say:

This candle is extinguished, but St Barbara's light is not. All women are goddesses, filled with strength!

December 16: FESTIVAL OF SAPIENTIA

Sapientia is the Roman goddess of wisdom and philosophy (similar to the Greek goddess Sophia). Celebrate her by reading, booking a course of study, organizing your bookshelf—physical or digital—or discussing a philosophical concept with your coven or friends and how it relates to Wicca, such as free will, substance theory, or intention. Eat some pomegranate, said to be the original "forbidden fruit" in the Bible as it held all knowledge and wisdom, and read tarot cards (or take a class in tarot if you are new to it).

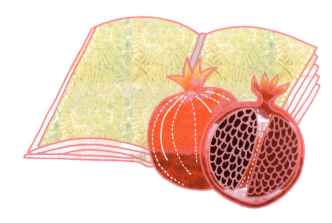

Sapientia ritual

Perform this ritual at night. Have some educational books around you, possibly even in the shape of a pentagram or as the circle around you if you have enough. Call the elements:

I call the element of Earth in the North, and ask it to nourish my need for knowledge!

I call the element of Air in the East, and ask it to bring me inspiration of what I must learn!

I call the element of Fire in the South, and ask it to fire up my quest for wisdom!

I call the element of Water in the West, and ask it to quench my thirst for knowledge!

Take a black scarf or piece of cloth and place it over your head. Say:

Darkness is here, darkness of night.

But it only obstructs mundane sight.

Through darkness and obstructions, I can see,

I can learn and have all knowledge important to me!

Remove the scarf and open your eyes slowly. Pick up the first book your eyes fall upon and read some of it while having a hot drink to symbolize your thirst for knowledge warming your mind and body.

December 24: CELTIC TREE MONTH OF BIRCH BEGINS

The black and white bark of the birch symbolizes the end of darkness, the birth of the Sun God at Yule, and light (white bark) taking over. Tie a red ribbon around a birch tree to ward off negative energy and give you positive energy for endeavors as the Sun grows stronger.

CHAPTER 4

Everyday Rituals

The best and most powerful rituals are those that you write yourself, or at least personalize. This chapter will show you how to do that, and also add some examples and inspiration for short and easy rituals that can become part of daily life—not every feast needs to be a big deal! To a witch, every day and every act is magical.

Performing Rituals

You have just read three chapters of rituals, so why do you need this chapter? Well, even if you want to carry out a ritual exactly according to the instructions given here, you need to prepare for it yourself, and by performing it, you will make it your own. This is important because it infuses the ritual with your own energy and gives it your individual power, making it more successful.

Preparing for a ritual

Preparing for a ritual can be as simple as walking out into your garden or a park. But it can also be elaborate, especially for Sabbats and life rituals. Here are some considerations:

- Location: Can you (and any guests or other participants) get there easily? While having a handfasting on top of a mountain could be awesome, if you want your elderly grandma there, you may want to choose a flatter space only a few steps away from where a car can park. If you are having it in a park, check that the park is open on the day and time you want to have it there—you do not want to get in trouble with the police! If it is indoors, is there enough space for everyone to be comfortable? What is nearby? The place may be nice looking, but is it beside a noisy factory so you will not be able to hear the ritual chanting, or by a smelly road full of traffic?
- Who will be there? There are two things to consider—people and place. Does the ritual just involve you? If not, how experienced are the people who you are inviting at participating or watching a witchy ritual? Some attendees with experience may love doing certain parts of a ritual, like calling the elements, so let them. Non-witches may be comfortable with being guests but might not want to read a Pagan poem or call the elements with you—equally, they may be happy to help! If you are in a public place, be that a park, a community room in the library, or the upstairs of a bar, can people just walk in? It is important to adjust your ritual to the comfort level of all who are there, even if they just happen upon your ritual; yes, we have religious freedom, and should not be afraid to practice witchcraft wherever we want, but we also do not want to scare people.

Once you have figured out the basics, it's time for the details. Make sure your space is clean—vacuum your living room and pick up trash outside (a good service to Mother Nature!). If you feel there is any negative energy or stress, use smudging or sprinkle a mix of mineral or clean well water and lemon juice around to clean out malevolent spirits and bad energy before the ritual starts.

Get the decorations you need as listed alongside each ritual. If you have limited access to witchy shops or online supply stores, no worries! Stock up around Halloween (cauldrons and witchy clothing) and Christmas (pentagrams and candles) in normal shops, or adapt everyday objects: a witchy broom can be a normal reed broom; plain white candles can become elemental or goddess candles by coloring them with a crayon, tying a ribbon of a specific color around them, or setting them in a suitable candleholder; table salt or wild flowers and leaves can represent Mother Earth; and so on.

The date and time of a ritual

Some rituals have specific dates when they should be performed, while others are supposed to be done at dawn or dusk, which gives them more energy (which is why that time was settled on after millennia of practice), but that does not mean if you oversleep or are still at work at dusk that you have to skip it. Wiccans aren't super picky and usually rituals such as Sabbats are fine to be done within three days of the official date, or the weekend before or after. We all have busy work and family lives, and the Goddess will not ignore you just because you have not carried out a ritual at a specific time!

When to do rituals without a specific time or date depends on the ritual and what suits those attending. For example, for rituals where you try to lessen an issue, you'd usually pick a waning moon—as the moon gets smaller in the sky, so will your issue. For rituals to make things grow, a waxing moon might be better—as the moon grows, so your idea, family, etc. will grow. If you are in a coven, they usually meet within three days of a full moon for monthly rituals, with some also meeting around the new moon for less formal rituals and teaching and for learning from each other. If your ritual is a big life ritual with many attendees, then you may go with a personal date, such as the anniversary of your first date for a wedding, or simply a date that suits everyone, and that is totally fine.

PERFORMING RITUALS

Adapting rituals

Witchcraft has no bible, and no rules that must be followed exactly. Even if you think what I have written is perfect, adapting rituals—from this book or others—is a good mental exercise and training for when you feel ready to write your own rituals. Sometimes you might think a ritual is great and perform it as written, but afterwards something feels "off" or the ritual does not work; try adapting it next time.

You can easily adapt the rituals to suit your personal circumstances too:

- Who are you? Most of the rituals here reference women, because witchcraft is somewhat female-focused. But if you identify as male or non-binary, you can absolutely adapt the rituals—try replacing some goddesses with gods or non-gendered spirits.
- What if you cannot be in the same place as your coven or family? You can perform virtual rituals instead! Agree on using the same words for calling the elements and each say them separately in your own homes, or you could split it up with the person who lives most in the south calling Fire, the most western person calling Water, and so on, all while live on a video chat. You could also write the ritual together beforehand, each set up a little altar in front of the camera, and all be in sync for the ritual. Once you've finished your ritual, you can all have "cakes and ale" and talk online.

RELAY RITUALS

If you're performing a virtual ritual, you could also perform it "relay style," as I have done a couple of times. Video yourself starting the ritual and saying one part, then send the god and goddess candles you've used to the next person in the ritual. This person records their part, then sends the candles to the next person, and so on. Once the whole ritual is recorded, splice all the clips together somewhere that you can all view them, such as on a private YouTube channel.

- Are you alone or with others? If you find a group ritual you like, but you do not have a coven, or if there is a solitary ritual you want to perform with friends—again, no problem! If you want to do a group ritual alone, and you feel you cannot do everything, you could prepare parts of the ritual ahead of time—perhaps record them and then play them when you do the main ritual—or simply omit them. If you want to perform a solitary ritual with a group, just split up the different parts of the ritual, such as calling the elements, asking the Goddess for guidance, thanking the elements at the end, and so on, or if no one wants to take the lead, write the parts on pieces of paper and pull them out of a hat.
- Who are you celebrating? Witchcraft embraces and accommodates all. If you cannot walk around the circle to call the elements, use a wheelchair or just turn a little while standing or sitting down. The handfasting in this book is written for a man and a woman, but all you need to change are the pronouns if you are a gay couple, or if you are in a poly-relationship, add an extra person and a longer ribbon so there is enough to tie three hands.
- Add and subtract! Always feel free to add your own chants, your favorite pieces of music, or perhaps a guided meditation into the ritual. Remove bits you do not feel comfortable with or that make the ritual too long for you. You can also mix and match—take the "calling the elements" wording from one ritual, the "requesting Mother Nature's aid" from a second, and the "calling down the moon" from a third. This is about YOU and what works for YOU.

Writing your own rituals

I find it easiest to write rituals in the same way as writing a food recipe.
- First, make a list of ingredients needed for the ritual, both physical (for example, candles or a goddess statue) and mental (how you want to call the elements and what chants to use), and name any preconditions (such as that the ritual should be performed on a certain day of the week, or during a certain moon phase).
- Then make a bullet-point list of what to do during the actual ritual, step by step, not forgetting even the small steps, such as lighting a candle—it will make quite a difference to a ritual's energy and magical intent whether a candle is lit throughout the ritual or whether the candle should be lit only at the end in order to burn something in its flame. Similarly, explain what to do with any other ingredients listed: should an herb just sit on the altar, or be burnt? If salt or sugar will be sprinkled around another object, such

as a photo or candle, should this be done clockwise (to gain something or increase energy) or counterclockwise (to lose something or diminish energy)?
- Say any vocal components out loud to yourself: do they "feel" right? Do you think they would flow better if they were wordier, and get you more in the right mood if they rhymed? Many rituals' vocal components rhyme: this is partially because it is tradition, but also because rhymes are more pleasing to the ear, are easier to memorize, and can help with the energy of the ritual, especially when chanted in a group.

KEEPING YOUR OWN BOOK OF SHADOWS

In the old days, each witch had a personal grimoire or Book of Shadows which was full of rituals, seasonal observances, and spells. Often, after a new member was initiated in a coven, he or she was then given access to the High Priestess' Book of Shadows and was expected to copy selected parts—or maybe all of it—by hand. Many witches these days still have something like it, because there is something very special, and very spiritual, in writing your own rituals by hand into a book. If you choose to have a paper Book of Shadows, I would strongly recommend writing your new ritual down on a loose piece of paper or in a notebook first. That way you can make changes if after the first time you perform the ritual, you feel it should be done at a different day of the week or a different chant should be used.

Of course, we live in the modern world and one of the great things about witchcraft is that it seamlessly integrates tradition and ancient wisdom with modern knowledge and abilities. So, many witches keep their Book of Shadows on their computer these days.

Daily Rituals

Daily rituals are small and unassuming, and often not overtly witchy—you likely already perform some without knowing. Do you always hit the snooze button twice before getting up, put on your socks before your pants, and brush your teeth before buttoning your shirt? That's a ritual. Do you always add sugar to your tea or coffee, stir clockwise five circles, then add milk and watch it swirl into the tea? That is a ritual, too!

With daily rituals, you can adapt what you do naturally, or write a ritual to suit your daily routine. For the above "getting up in the morning" example, you may say a prayer of thanks as you hit the snooze button, visualize putting on spiritual and energetic armor as you get dressed to protect yourself from negativity and bad people throughout your day, and say a chant in your head about saying kind words, being patient with people, and not biting their head off as you brush your teeth. With the tea/coffee example, visualize stirring energy for yourself for the rest of the day into the tea, and the milk being the blessing from the Moon Goddess; you could add a few counterclockwise (called widdershins in Wicca) stirs to remove negative energy and stress from yourself.

This section includes some quick and fun daily rituals to help make your day better in small ways.

Cleaning ritual

This ritual can be done anytime you have a shower or bath, or even when you wash your hands. Take a few deep breaths and nod to north, south, east, and west—representing the four elements. As you wash yourself, visualize stress and worry about the day washing off you like dirt, leaving behind only a calm, energized you.

Try to use soap or bath bubbles with ingredients related to the magical aim of the ritual, such as peppermint to see a problem clearly, orange for more energy and justice, cinnamon for vigor and passion, or basil for financial success. Say a few words or a short chant while you are washing to ask for the deities' help and blessing.

Way-to-work ritual

An easy way to be mindful of your witchy side and make your commute via car or train less mundane is to call the elements on your way to work and thank them for any assistance on the way back, thus making your whole day an informal ritual! Keep a little salt in your car to sprinkle over your shoulder for Earth, hang a car air freshener (or even better, natural potpourri or something scented with essential oils) for Air, make a quick flame with a lighter (if allowed) or rub your hands together to make them warm for Fire, and drink some water (or coffee!) for Water. You could also play "I spy… the elements"—look out the window to watch the wind bending trees and blowing trash about, see the local river or any lakes, and so on.

Calling the parking fairy

Carry some spare chocolate in your car. When you need a parking space on a busy street, drive clockwise around the area and chant:

Parking fairy I am in a bind,

But a parking space I will find!

Once you have parked, drop a piece of chocolate by the curb with thanks to the parking fairy.

Magical cooking

Anytime you cook or bake, it is part of a ritual which honors Mother Earth's bounty and nourishes yourself and your loved ones. Make it even more so by calling the elements as you cook (Earth as you gather ingredients, Air when your cooking's aromas reach your nose and you see steam, Fire when you turn on the stove, Water when you fill the pan with water). Then call on a suitable deity to assist and bless the meal, such as hunter goddess Diana if you have venison or fish, the Sun God when you add carrots or oranges, or Hecate when adding black pepper and cloves, knowing they bust negativity and bad luck. Say a prayer of thanks to Mother Nature before you sit down to eat, then thank the elements when you clean up.

Sleep time

Sleep is so important. Lack of it can make you ill, so having both a mundane and magical sleep ritual can be crucial to your physical and mental health. On the mundane side, make sure to slow down about an hour before bed, minimize electronics and light in the bedroom, and have a calming drink such as chamomile or hot milk with honey before bed.

Magically, get a pale blue piece of cloth (blue for calm and healing), and some lavender and chamomile—blossoms are ideal, but essential oils work too. Call on the goddess Posithea, Greek goddess of rest, to attend you and watch over your sleep. Sit or lie comfortably and slow your breathing. Add the blossoms or oils to the cloth and say:

Stress, go away, worries vanish!

Bad energy I banish!

I lay down to sleep,

It will be restful and deep!

Fold up the cloth with the lavender and chamomile blossoms/oils and place it under your pillow.

Weekly Rituals

Weekly rituals tend to be a mix of the mundane and the truly magical and more formal rituals, and they are often carried out on specific days of the week suitable for the intent of the ritual (such as Tuesday for justice, Sunday for gaining extra energy, or Saturday for ending things and banishing negativity). They can be repeated weekly to build up energy until the aim is achieved. You can make taking out the trash a small weekly ritual by remembering it probably contains a little of all four elements—old food for Earth, smelly stuff for Air, ashes and burned food for Fire, and liquids and soggy items for Water. As you take out the trash, visualize taking out bad habits and negativity, too, and removing them from your home, which is the ultimate ritual space and sacred circle. Similarly, if you iron clothes once a week, do a meditative ritual during that time; or when changing the bed linen, cast a circle first, then see the changing of the bed as an opportunity to bring fresh energy and hope of change of anything stale or negative in your life.

It is also important to schedule time each week specifically for your magical practice. I am not one for routines for my family in general, but both my husband and I have prescheduled "alone times"—his are mostly for watching football, mine are for magic. These scheduled slots do not always need to be hours at a time—you can use them for a short ritual to get energy and the gods' protection for the upcoming week on a Sunday evening, a prayer for the deities' guidance as you look at your schedule for the week, or a ritual performed in your head calling the elements, conversing with the deities, doing a guided meditation, and thanking the elements all while you sit waiting for your child's weekly ballet lesson to be over.

Nature ritual

Make time for nature at least once a week—preferably more often, of course, depending on your schedule and the weather. Go for a walk in the fields or forest, or even the grass verge along a street. Notice the four elements naturally present in nature or look for colors corresponding to the elements (green/brown for Earth, white/yellow for Air, red/orange for Fire, and blue for Water). Take a rest against a tree, visualizing the branches reaching up to the Sun God and the roots down to Mother

Nature, and if you have time, do a meditation to calm and reset your busy life. Then ask nature deities for guidance and their blessings—for example, the Egyptian goddess Geb, the Celtic goddess Abnoba, or the Norse god Tapio. Look for signs of an answer as you start walking toward home, such as finding a penny, which could symbolize that you will have more money soon, or the wind changing direction, which may hint you should perhaps move or look for a job in that direction.

Money ritual

Thursday is good for money magic. Combine the mundane and magical management of money with this little ritual. Make sure your front door is free of obstructions that could stop money energy and perhaps add a basil plant near it. Call the elements, placing a coin in each elemental direction, and light a green candle on your altar, then making a pentagram with coins around it. Say:

Money, money come to me.

Financial opportunities with this ritual I'll see.

I don't ask for much—just money for food, fun, and such!

Then spend some time paying bills, checking your bank accounts for fraudulent activities, or looking for a side hustle or new venture that could bring in some cash, before moving your coin pentagram to under your doormat, and thanking the elements for money they are bringing into the household.

WEEKLY RITUALS **135**

Hump day ritual

Wednesday is often called "hump day," as it is in the middle of the week. It's also the best day for communication rituals. Visualize the four elements, and schedule any difficult meetings or discussions with your partner on that day, as you are more likely to come to an understanding. Light a white candle or place a covert white pentagram nearby (as a wall decoration, worn as jewelry, or made with four white pens) to increase peaceful energies.

Love ritual

Love rituals are traditionally performed on Friday, the day of love goddess Venus, but can also be done on a Sunday (for the Sun God) if you are a male or looking for a man, or Monday (for the Moon Goddess) if you want to enhance your female goddess energies and self-love or are looking for a woman.

Call the elements, asking them to bring you love and remove obstacles to finding it. Take a candle—pink for romantic love or red for lustful/sexual love—and carve a heart into it. You can also add words, such as the three main qualities you are looking for in a partner, or if you want to strengthen existing love, write the name of your partner. You could write the words above the heart so they energize and disappear first when the candle is lit, or below it so they remind you of what you are looking for in love even when the ritual is finished.

Light the candle, then sprinkle a little salt (for Earth) and water onto the candle, which already represents Fire and Air (from the smoke), and remind yourself that it is important to be balanced in yourself to receive love, and to balance giving and receiving love. Drop a few drops of wax onto a piece of rose quartz and carry the crystal with you wherever you go. Keep repeating this ritual weekly until the heart is no longer visible on the candle.

EVERYDAY RITUALS

Monthly Rituals

Monthly rituals are usually bigger than daily or weekly ones, and include Esbats (see below) and rituals that take longer and need more preparation; these rituals may build up energy over several months, up to a year or more. A common long-term ritual is a "blue moon ritual," from one blue moon—the second of two full moons in a month—to the next, which is over two years on average. Examples may be rituals to find and keep balance in your life, to keep a harmonious environment at work, or to repair a relationship with your in-laws. Of course, there are also other rituals you might do monthly, such as rituals that need time to gather power throughout the month, rituals related to your monthly menstrual cycle, or general blessing and protection rituals that are renewed every month.

Esbats

Wiccans have a monthly ritual called an Esbat every full moon. Esbats provide an opportunity to meet and socialize with other witches, learn from each other, and make magic together that may be difficult or not as powerful when done alone. In the past, Esbats were held on the full moon because the rituals had to be kept secret and communication was difficult, but everyone knew when the full moon was. As the power of the full moon lasts several days, it is perfectly acceptable to carry out your Esbat a couple of days either side of the complete full moon, if that better suits your work or family commitments.

Follow these steps for your own Esbat ritual, which can be done on your own or with a group.

Cast a circle by saying:

As above, so below, as without, so within, as the universe, so my soul, as the world, so my mind. The circle is cast and I am beyond the worlds beyond the bounds of time, where night and day, birth and death, joy and sorrow meet as one.

Invite the elements:

From the North, I call forth Earth, which is grounded strength. Hail and welcome!

From the East, I call forth Air, which is clear thought. Hail and welcome!

From the South, I call forth Fire, which is vital spirit. Hail and welcome!

From the West, I call forth Water, which is intuitive wisdom. Hail and welcome!

Invoke the God and Goddess (often symbolized by a silver or white candle for the Goddess, and gold or black for the God):

O Goddess who rules Earth and all within, who sets the time our lives begin, who brings me happiness and mirth, who gives me value and self-worth: touch this circle with your love, as below me, so above!

O God of the Sun that shines above, who warms us with your light and love, who brings good health and prosperity and changes all as it should be: touch this circle with your love, as below me, so above!

Light the altar candles and say:

We light this candle today in presence of the Lord and Lady, without malice, without jealousy, without envy, without fear of aught beneath the setting sun, for we know that their light and love will guide us down the right path, even when we cannot see it, even in the darker times of winter ahead.

This wording is usually used because, in the old times, winter was the biggest threat to your family, animals, and food sources, but there is nothing wrong with adapting it if you prefer, saying something like "even in the darker times and during any trouble ahead."

Take some time to center and think about what you want to do this month. This ritual also provides a good time to bless new gems or magical jewelry, read some spiritual poems, or work on spells.

When you are finished, move on to the "cakes and ale" part of the ritual, where you eat and drink something seasonal to ground yourself, have some social time if you are in a coven, and connect to nature via food and drink. Then release the elements, deities, and circle by thanking them.

Cleansing ritual

Just as there are household tasks that you do once a month, so there are magical rituals, and cleansing your home (and workplace, if you can do it covertly) and protecting it is one of them. This ritual will remove negative energy from stress and fights, and protect your home from others' bad intentions, break-ins, and other negativity.

Smudge your home by walking around the house counterclockwise with bundles of smoldering dry sage, paying particular attention that smoke gets into corners and any areas where people have had an argument or have been ill.

Now chant the following words:

Badness, badness go away! You are not allowed to here stay!

You can also ring a bell to remove ghosts and negative energies. Only once this is complete, call the elements in your favorite way (see page 8).

Light an altar candle in white (for pure energy) or a color corresponding to your patron deity and ask them to protect your home. Eat some food to strengthen you and symbolize the blessing of the deities.

Mix some salt with black peppercorns, cloves, or clove oil, and add a little pure water from a spring or river to make it into a paste. Pass the paste over the altar candle to bless it, and then spread a little on windowsills and door jambs, going clockwise around your home, to protect your home and those living in it from evil, both spiritual and physical.

Return to your altar, and dismiss the elements, thanking them for their assistance in keeping you and yours safe.

Promotion ritual

If you are working toward a promotion at work, you need to be patient. You may think you cannot really perform magic at work, but you can! Rituals do not all involve loud chanting and lighting candles.

Invite the elements in your head, or symbolize them with office supplies, like pens, paperclips, or a mix of staplers, scissors, rulers, and so on—choose items in colors associated with the elements if possible (for example, a red stapler for Fire, scissors with a blue handle for Water, a brown wooden ruler for Earth, and a travel-size deodorant for Air). Then make a pentagram with those office supplies on your desk. Next, bring up a picture of a god or goddess on your phone or computer and ask them for help gaining the promotion, and why you want it. Repeat this monthly on a waxing moon, until you get that job!

Resources

www.facebook.com/SiljasGreenWiccan
My Facebook page, regularly updated with news and other links of interest.

www.learnreligions.com/paganism-wicca-4684806
This website has great, unbiased info on Wicca and specific sections for sabbats, rituals, and the Celtic Tree Months.

www.shirleytwofeathers.com/The_Blog/pagancalendar/pagan-calendar-2/monthly-calendar
Monthly calendar with even more small festivals and rituals than are in this book.

www.atcwicca.org
Great American Wiccan website.

www.circlesanctuary.org
Circle Sanctuary: author and famous Wiccan Selena Fox's website and organization with information on life rituals, events, interfaith work, and more.

www.cog.org
Covenant of the Goddess: this mostly US-based group works on getting legal recognition for Wicca and is very active in networking.

www.paganfed.org
The Pagan Federation: an international organization, UK based, that runs witchy events and also has a great magazine.

www.witchcraft.org
The Children of Artemis: UK-based organization with an informative website. They also run witchy gatherings and conventions and publish a magazine.

www.sacred-texts.com
Religious and spiritual texts, including Wiccan, Pagan, and Druid.

GLOSSARY

Athame A ritual knife that is not used to cut things physically, but for magic and working with energy, such as dipping the tip of the blade in a bowl of herbs on the altar to charge them with magical energy for future use in spells or medicinal teas. Traditionally has a black handle.

Bolline Knife used to cut things used for magic such as herbs or cord. Traditionally has a white handle.

Book of Shadows A diary for a witch to write down spells and magic; often kept online these days. Abbreviated to BoS.

Cauldron A large pot or bowl, traditionally black, used to make magical foods and for water-scrying.

Celtic Tree calendar A Celtic/witchy version of astrology. There are 13 Celtic tree months in a year, originally based on lunar months but now linked to fixed dates.

Coven A group of witches working magic together regularly.

Divination Reading the future with tarot cards, runes, or other methods.

Elements Each of the four elements, Air, Fire, Water, and Earth, are linked to particular colors and directions. This is often symbolized in rituals through using candles in those colors placed in the corresponding positions.

ELEMENT	COLOR	DIRECTION
Earth	brown or green	North
Air	yellow or white	East
Fire	red or orange	South
Water	blue	West

Familiar Animal, often a pet, who helps in magic.

Gods and Goddesses There are many gods and goddesses in mythology (such as Celtic, Greek, or Roman). But there is also the concept of God for male energy/all male deities and Goddess for female energy/all female deities/goddess power in women.

High Priest(ess) Coven leader and teacher.

Pagan Originally any believer in non-monotheistic religion, but these days usually means a believer in Earth-based spirituality (such as Wiccan, Druid, or Shaman).

Patron deity Like a more powerful guardian angel, this is a god or goddess you feel especially close to at this time in your life.

Quarter candles Another name for elemental candles; *see also* Elements.

Pentacle A five-pointed star in a circle. Sometimes a five-petaled flower is used to symbolize this on the altar, or a pentagram is made from stalks of herbs.

Pentagram A five-pointed star without a circle, although the term is often used interchangeably with pentacle.

Sigil A magical symbol, often personally designed.

Smudging A method of spiritual cleansing to remove negativity, performed by burning herbs (often sage) and allowing the smoke to waft through areas and over items in need of cleansing.

Visualization Imagining something in your mind's eye. Also used for very deep meditation.